Cobwebs, Echoes and Footprints

Cobwebs, Echoes and Footprints

A Collection of Stories and Memories

ReadersMagnet, LLC

Cobwebs, Echoes and Footprints: A Collection of Stories and Memories
Copyright © 2019 by Robert Easton

Published in the United States of America
ISBN Paperback: 978-1-950947-57-7
ISBN eBook: 978-1-950947-58-4

All rights reserved. No part of this publication may be reproduced, stored in a retrieval system or transmitted in any way by any means, electronic, mechanical, photocopy, recording or otherwise without the prior permission of the author except as provided by USA copyright law.

The opinions expressed by the author are not necessarily those of ReadersMagnet, LLC.

ReadersMagnet, LLC
10620 Treena Street, Suite 230 | San Diego, California, 92131 USA
1.619.354.2643 | www.readersmagnet.com

Book design copyright © 2019 by ReadersMagnet, LLC. All rights reserved.
Cover design by Ericka Walker
Interior design by Shemaryl Evans

Dedication

This collection is dedicated to the memory of Miss Geneva Dreskell, my first grade teacher, Miss Jennie West and all my other elementary school teachers who pinched my earlobes and taught me to love woods and storybooks, and to all librarians everywhere.

In Remembrance

This special tribute is for my only sister who was born October 29th, 1929 and died on February 24th, 2006. Her name was Margaret Elizabeth Prindle Easton and her life was largely an unlived life because of her long battle against multiple sclerosis.

Prior to her slowly debilitating condition and confinement in institutions for most of her adult life, she nevertheless was Valedictorian of her high school class in 1948, graduated from college, married, had two children, one grand-daughter, and was a legal secretary and a high school teacher who taught fine arts and home economics.

To say she had colossal potential is an understatement because she was a creative entity and it makes me sad to think she never got her "fifteen minutes of fame" or even a chance to stand in the batter's box.

Robert D. Easton
2009

Acknowledgments

"Raintrap Conflict" was first published in a slightly altered version by the Hibiscus Press of Sacramento, California in the Winter 1975 issue of their literary magazine, In A Nutshell.

"Fantasy In Half-Way Land" was originally published by the Hibiscus Press in the Winter 1976 issue of their literary magazine, In A Nutshell.

"My Lost Love" was first published in the September 1974 issue of The National Humane Review.

My special thanks to Marilyn Pribus and Mary Alice Coverdale for their invaluable help with editing and proofreading chores in this and previous works.

About the Author

Robert D. Easton is a native of the state of Washington. He earned two liberal arts degrees from Central Washington State College at Ellensburg, Washington and has done post-graduate work at colleges in California.

Although a veteran of the Korean War, he served in Europe as well as in Stateside army posts as a teletype operator and message center clerk for the U.S. Army Signal Corps during 1953 and 1954.

At various periods in his life, he has worked as a custodian, section hand, truck driver, newspaper reporter, schoolteacher, technical writer, landscape technician, parks maintenance worker, nurseryman, salesman, public school classified employee, warehouseman, and computer assembler. He is currently employed as a test evaluator for Kelly Services at CTB/McGraw-Hill, Mather, California.

He placed 22nd (out of 100) in the 1974 Writer's Digest Article Contest and has written nonfiction articles for Air California, National Humane Review, Horse and Rider, Sacramento Magazine, and Good Old Days magazines. The Hibiscus Press (In A Nutshell), a literary magazine, has published four of his short stories.

In May, 1978, he self–published a book of nostalgia entitled Tales from the Palouse Country and in 2004 a memoir entitled Beyond the Palouse.

For 300 days in 1979, He circumnavigated the globe in the "world's smallest cruise ship", the windjammer "Yankee Trader." He is currently writing a lengthy account of that voyage.

He lives in Sacramento and has four grown children and six grandchildren.

Contents

Introduction 15

PART ONE: FICTION

Raintrap Conflict 19
Fantasy in Half–Way Land 26
The Watermelon Dream 35
Homer's Lament 43
A Prayer for Josie 49
Roger's Trip 52
Patterns in Paradise 54
Francis with an "I" 59
Angela and Gloria 63
Dogwood Memory 72

PART TWO: MEMOIRS

Freedom Train Revisited 81
My Lost Love 85
Airport Incident 87
The Hospital Experience 92
On The Nature of Horses 98

The Conference Mystique 102
Why I Don't Ski Anymore 106
A Journey into No–Man's World 109
The Bear Saga 112
A Day on a Nude Beach 118
Shasta Mountain High 124
Notes From A Backpacker 128
Nature in the Raw 133
Looking Back at Vanishing Wild Places 138
How Not To Kill a Cat 144

Introduction

Writing was never more than a hobby to me–just as reading was and still is. I enjoy them both immensely. As for writing, I was never disciplined or professional. I did it when it suited my mood. It was always a part–time thing and fulfilled my creative needs as I squeezed it in while working for a living. Writing was always attempted during and between marriages, divorces, the subsequent child–rearing years and dead–end jobs.

What follows are short pieces and memoirs placed pretty much in the order that I wrote and lived them. That makes them dated and possibly redundant but I like to call them stories; at the very least they are vignettes wrapped around character sketches. Some are "slices of life."

The fiction covers a broad range of subjects and is written from different points of view in more than the "third–person" style. My ideas came from my imagination and dreams and also from watching people, eavesdropping on them and reading a wide variety of material from other writers. My prose reveals many of the human foibles with which I have grappled during my adult life.

Many of these pieces do not have happy endings and some of them are about "losers" because it is unrealistic to think that everyone is a winner in life or in any other endeavor.

Most people want to relate to winners; therefore, my stories probably won't make folks feel good, offer hope to the multitudes, provide information or teach anybody how to do something. I do hope they are entertaining.

The male characters in the first two stories and the last story are meant to represent some of the problems many men face today such as loss of identity, age–related health problems, marital issues, male menopause, struggles to climb corporate ladders, and trying to come to grips with their own mortality.

As for the memoirs, they are random rambling rantings of an" aspiring" reclusive wealthy literary genius who longs to live a "writer's life." The only one published was "My Lost Love" in the National Humane Review in 1974.

Most of these works, including some of the memoirs, have been submitted to periodicals at least once. Unfortunately, they never found a home anywhere. Perhaps they have major irreversible flaws in them.

Robert D. Easton
2009

PART ONE

FICTION

Raintrap Conflict

On that particular rainy Saturday afternoon, Murray Brundage had just turned on the television and settled back in his recliner when his wife issued the ultimatum.

"Murray, I've been patient long enough! All this year I agreed to be a football widow but good grief, now baseball! If you don't forget those ball games and clean the attic and garage today, I swear I'm going back to mother!"

Even though he knew she wasn't really mad, her eyes flashed warning daggers, and he realized this time he was trapped.

He rose regretfully from his chair thinking how ridiculous it would be for his middle-aged wife to leave him after twenty-five years of marriage and move in with her bitchy mother in that apartment across town.

"Aw, Flo, don't be like that! This is the last game of the World Series."

"Murray, you know how moody you get after those games. I don't see why you want to keep making yourself miserable but maybe you'll have time to see part of it later. Now get at those jobs, Buster, and I'm not kidding!"

When they first married, they had agreed that Murray would do the outside "man-type" work and Flo would manage the house.

Technically, then, the garage and attic, being part of the house, were Flo's domain but Murray thought he'd better not mention that fact now.

The system hadn't worked too well because Murray spent more than one weekend helping rearrange furniture. It evened out, though, because in the months following Murray's first knee operation, Flo had to do everything.

Suddenly grasping a new escape plan, Murray asked, "Where's the kid? It wouldn't hurt him to help out a little around here."

"John's in his room cramming for exams but it's your job, anyway, so get going, Murray!"

Murray went to the hall closet, slipped on his sweater and slowly moved his ponderous bulk toward the garage door. He stopped on the way to pick up his can of beer from the coffee table.

Sheets of rain thundered on the garage roof and pelted the windows as he surveyed the chaos of boxes, tools, and sporting goods.

Sipping his beer, be began picking up tools with one hand and remembering he'd been through this before, this shuffling and burying, this stuffing of nondescript items into boxes shoved into dark corners.

Why hadn't he built cabinets and organized storage areas? Was it the cost or was that just a flimsy excuse? He always felt so tired. Or was it just laziness? It seemed that he never had time. But then, why couldn't he hire the work done?

Murray pondered these questions only momentarily and, just as in other days, filled and closed the boxes, took a last look around, hastily swept the floor around the cars and the boat and told himself he was finished.

On his way back through the kitchen, Murray paused long enough to drop his empty beer can into the garbage bin, opened the fridge for a fresh six-pack, and grabbed some potato chips.

As he started clown the hall and up the stairs, he noticed he was breathing fast. He couldn't help remembering when he could easily run up that staircase, two steps at a time.

It seemed only yesterday but then, what the hell, there was still time to get back in shape. Fifty wasn't old. A little exercise and he'd he fit again!

At the landing, he hesitated, hearing the piercing sounds of a modern rock band. Would John really be bent over his desk, pouring over textbooks? How could he study in all that racket?

Impulsively, Murray knocked on the door and barged in without waiting for John's response.

John was lying on his bed, a book in his hands. With one quick movement, he put his right hand under the covers and sat up.

Slapped in the face with the sweet smell of marijuana, Murray chose to ignore the odor because he knew not only years separated him from his son. His own permissiveness and a drug-oriented society had also widened the gap.

Why did he find it so difficult to talk to this long-haired stranger? Who was this twenty-year-old savage bent on saving the world?

Ten years had slipped by quickly but he and John still had some things in common, Murray thought. They both worked for the same company, didn't they? So what if he was a foreman and John was on the assembly line? It was all the same, wasn't it? The manufacture of plastics. What was so bad about that? It was as good a job as any. Try to tell John that. He either flared back about being exploited by the establishment or skulked away in silence.

"Hey, John," Murray yelled, "mind turning that off. I'd like to talk to you for a minute."

John slowly brought his left hand out from under the covers and reached to lower the volume.

"Sure, Dad, what do you want?"

"Your mother tells me you're cramming. I'd hoped you could take some time out to help me clean the attic." Expecting an instant recoil, Murray added quickly, "Care for a beer?"

Murray thought: Why do I hate drugs yet allow John to use them in my house? Why do I reject his use of dope yet I offer him alcohol? How big a hypocrite can one man be?

John smiled slowly, took the can, wiped the top with his palm and said, "Gosh, Dad, I'm swamped. Studying for these tests has got to come ahead of a cluttered attic."

Murray felt a flush of anger and said icily, "John, I know how you feel about manual labor but dammit kid, I think I deserve some help. Your mother and I can't do it all. We've worked hard to give you a decent life and I've spent fifteen years in that plant so you could get a better education than I did. And before that, I did anything I could to put food on the table."

John sprang from the bed and faced Murray defiantly.

"Dad, if you force me to do housework, I'll get the hell out of here. It's a waste of my time and brains. How many times do I have to tell you I don't want the same things out of life you do? You're a materialist with those capitalistic security symbols and you resent me because I'm not money hungry like you!"

Murray felt himself shrink under John's gaze, awed by the piercing hot eyes, amazed at the way his son challenged him with the courage of a cornered rat.

Struggling to control his rage, Murray managed to say in hushed tones, "You'll learn someday, John, that it isn't all in the books. Of course I want you to get an education but it helps to know how to work with your hands, too. I don't want you to spend your life hitch-hiking up and down the freeways like those other bums. Sure, I could have been more successful if I had finished college, but I didn't do too badly at that."

"What do you mean you didn't do too badly?" John screamed. "Where are you? Stuck in a dead-end job with nowhere to go. I don't want to end up like you. I've been meaning to tell you. I'm quitting the plant and maybe these crummy college courses, too. I'd like to chuck it all and travel awhile. I can't stand it anymore and I'll tell you why. I'm bored, get that? Bored! And I think you are, too, but you won't admit it, even to yourself. Now, if you'll excuse me, I've got to get back to my studies."

Struck dumb, Murray retreated, closed the door behind him and stood shaking in the hallway. He thought about what John had said. Maybe the kid was right. Maybe he had been fooling himself. The work was deadly dull and he had reached a plateau. He'd been twice passed over for promotion and the only supervisory jobs left were going to highly educated and specialized guys who knew how to play politics.

Murray stopped musing long enough to gulp down his beer and attack the attic stairs. He was glad Flo wasn't there to see how he puffed as he headed up the stairway and flung open the attic door.

John's words rang in his ears as Murray stared at his image reflected in the gilded mirror hanging there in the gloom.

Murray thought back to this morning when he stood bare-chested before his shaving mirror downstairs. He remembered seeing the tired eyes staring back at him, the wrinkles he had been trying to erase with that expensive cream. He recalled the balding head, the ugly paunch, the whole sickening wreck of a man. Who says fifty isn't old?

The ugliness of the image made him whirl suddenly and the motion sent needles of pain shooting through his knee; the memory came back of the eternity of days spent in hospitals. Three operations and the pain was still there.

At the same time, his gaze fell upon the rain pounding against the small circular attic window, and he couldn't help thinking about that other rainy day so long ago.

It was those memories of that other rainy day that made him push through the bundles of clothes, reach upon a dusty shelf, and bring down a large wooden chest. He sipped his beer, wiped the moisture from his hands, and caressed the box. Gently, he dusted it off, eased it open.

He fondled the miniature baseball bats, the silver cups, the pennants, the faded photographs of his teammates. He touched the rotting leather of his second baseman's glove and brushed his fingers along the laces of the cleated shoes.

Then he saw the yellowed newspaper clipping and subhead reading, Brundage Injured. Why was his throat so tight he found it difficult to swallow?

Murray looked out the window again. Suddenly, he was back in 1946 at the end of another World Series. In the seventh inning he had wrenched his right knee while trying to tag a base runner and in the eighth had smashed the same knee on a slide into third.

Then, it was the bottom of the ninth, their last chance at bat, one run behind, bases loaded, two outs, and he was up. The bleachers were full of screaming fans despite the pouring rain.

Painfully, he had stood in the batter's box as the count reached two and one, then three balls and two strikes and finally, that fatal fast ball which he swung at and missed. They had to carry him to the locker room.

With a choking lump in his throat and a wetness in his eyes, Murray winced as he heard footsteps on the landing.

Then Flo's voice came up the stairs, closer and with an ever louder, "Murray! Aren't you finished yet? Mur–ray?"

Quickly covering the open chest with a newspaper, he heard her voice coming closer, turned and saw Flo leaning against the doorjamb.

"Murray, have you forgotten we've got to go shopping this afternoon?"

Suddenly seeing the chest, she turned away and said, "I'm sorry, Murray, I didn't realize you were..." Then she turned back, reached out her hand to touch his shoulder, and slowly crept downstairs.

In her place in the doorway, John appeared. "Dad, I just want to say I'm sorry for the way I sounded off just now. I didn't mean it. I guess maybe I will stay in school, at least till the end of the year. We might disagree on some things but you're okay. You'll always be my father and I'll always be your son, no matter what. You lived your life the way you wanted and you played the game the way you saw it."

"John, I..." Murray started.

"I heard that last part in a movie once," John laughed, and then, "Sure. I'll help you with the attic. What do you want me to do first! Are you all right, Dad? You look kind of funny. Hey, are you crying?"

Awkwardly, Murray turned his face sideways and stifled a sob as he reached to embrace his son.

"I'm okay, kid. It's just this lousy dust up here. Gets in my eyes and throat, too. What do you say we have another beer before we get started? Let's hurry, maybe we can catch the last few innings!"

Far away to the west the rain had stopped, the skies were clearing and on the horizon a yellow sun floated in a cloudless blue.

Somewhere, beyond another distant horizon, an 18–year–old rookie slammed his first home run over the stadium fence.

Fantasy in Half-Way Land

Theodore J. Purvis wondered how other men spent their "night out" as he walked out of the theater after three hours of X-rated movies.

He thought about Alice and their marriage. He was lucky. Many husbands never got a night out, not even with "the boys."

Ted didn't have close men friends or lady friends either, and Alice didn't really feel a need for them to have friends. They had each other. That arrangement seemed to be the norm these days.

Alice must have wondered what he did when he was away from her but she rarely asked as long as he came home at a decent hour.

Still, seldom could he go away by himself on weekends. It wasn't that Alice wouldn't let him. She gave him plenty of freedom. Perhaps too much and he couldn't handle it.

After twenty years of marriage and four kids, other things came first. Things like mowing the lawn, the PTA, the kids' school activities, civic and social clubs and all the other enslaving duties that go with being a husband and father in the suburbs. Why was it so many great weekends were sacrificed for mundane chores?

Now it was a dreary Friday night in midwinter. The holidays were over and the streets were quiet, as if all the fun lovers had left the world forever. Actually, they were probably in San Francisco or Reno.

The movies had been an escape from his problems and as he reached the parking lot and climbed into his station wagon, he knew he had to talk to somebody about what had happened that day.

Lester, the barkeeper, would be his shoulder to cry on.

Thus, Ted drove to his favorite side street pub, knowing it would be the same as always. He would be alone in that dark corner, a double Scotch on the rocks, drinking bad booze after bad movies to give him another bad taste in his mouth.

Again, as always, the lounge was filled with bleary-eyed men sitting on counter stools who swung their heads only far enough to see who came in. Ted walked over to the bar.

Lester was behind the counter washing glasses. Perversely, Ted ordered brandy on the rocks instead of Scotch and said, "Well, Lester, old boy, you might as well be the last to know. I lost out again. Hugh Canby got the job and I got the shaft. I'm back to pushing a pencil and shuffling papers. They will not be giving me a new foot-long title and my name on the door."

"Sorry, Ted. Better luck next time. Maybe you should think about transferring to sales. All insurance salesmen make the big dough." Lester handed him his drink.

Lester didn't want to listen to Ted so he changed the subject. "My girl is off. Makes me short-handed tonight. Got to get ready to close." Ted retreated to his dark corner.

Lester cave the bar a quick wipe and turned back to his glasses.

Like everyone today, Ted thought, Lester didn't want to be involved, to get close to anyone. What did Lester know about the insurance business anyway? It didn't take brains to be an agent; a toothy smile and a firm handshake would do.

Ted sat in his corner, downed his drink, walked out and stood beside his big Ford wagon. A breeze blew a few drops of rain in his face.

He thought about how lonely he was and Alice couldn't understand how he could feel lonely in a city of five hundred thousand people. She didn't know the difference between being alone and being lonely. They both knew he wouldn't have time for an affair or anything like that.

Alice treated him like a little boy and thought he was silly when he told her sometimes he felt as though he was going to cry. Now was one of those times.

Why did he think so often about running away from the rat–race to a place in the sun, to act out his boyhood dreams of adventure? He had wanted to trek through the Andes, to sail a small boat to tropical islands, to travel through Austria during opera season. They were all half–baked wishes; none ever came true.

Why did he feel that life was passing him by? The first half or his life was gone; ahead lay the second half with old age, sickness, and finally death. He was alone in halfway land.

Then he saw a pretty girl weaving across the street toward him in the cheerless night. She wore blue jeans, a shawl over a white and black shirt, waffle stompers on her feet.

She came right up to his face. "Are you going downtown?" she asked.

He lied as he said, "I'm going in that direction."

He helped her into the front seat and she looked at him strangely as if it were odd that he'd hold the door for her. The heavy smell of cheap wine on her breath hit him full in the face.

He moved behind the wheel and she bounced over beside him, tucked her boot under her so that her left knee touched his side. He smiled with regret, thinking Alice had never done that even years ago when they were first dating.

In the girl's right hand was a paper bag which she opened, showing him three empty wine bottles and saying, "I'm sorry I look such a mess, but my brother beat me up and kicked me out. He said I was nothing but a tramp, and that's when I started drinking."

Tears were in her eyes and he replied as he thought some movie heartthrob like Clark Gable might. "Sorry to hear you've been having a bad time. What can I do to help?"

For an answer, she said in sobbing gasps, "Hey, I know of a friend's apartment downtown. Would you like to party with me tonight?"

He tried to be debonair when he said, "That sounds like fun."

Obviously, she loved wine and so he pulled into a liquor store and at her suggestion bought three bottles of a mediocre Chablis and her favorite brand of cigarettes.

When he got back into the wagon and they drove off, he noticed out of the corner of his eye that she seemed to be scrutinizing him with an intent stare as if trying to guess his age and sexual suitability.

While mounting the two flights of stairs to the apartment, he couldn't help thinking the two of them must have looked like Don Quixote and Dulcinea. With her unkempt black hair, she was a damsel in distress and he was her knight-errant, lover, and adventurer supreme.

Drifting in his daydream, lie stumbled on the shabby stairs and awoke, realizing how ridiculous the spectacle would have been to anyone seeing them. Like a scene from a play, Timid Ted Purvis, a forty-five-year-old insurance underwriter with a girl who told him she was nineteen years old.

What did she want with him? With premature thinning gray hair, eyeglasses and a paunch, he wasn't one to make a girl's heart beat faster. Maybe she had a father complex or saw him as a big brother who would be kind to her, or at the very least, someone to talk to. Could she be dumb enough to think he was wealthy? His vehicle didn't reflect that.

So here he was with a tawdry but pretty girl, bound for a possible night of love, picking fruit in never-never land. Was sex outside of marriage the last great adventure left to modern man? What would Alice think?

Inside the living room of the apartment, Ted was struck with bareness. Only huge pillows, mattresses, a lamp and a stereo.

The girl moved quickly into the kitchen and opened the refrigerator. He saw it was empty except for a tray of ice cubes. She shut the door and brought down two tall champagne flutes from a very dusty cupboard. She quickly and expertly opened a bottle of wine and poured the flutes full, then shoved the other two bottles back into the fridge.

They touched their glasses together as if in a toast and drank deeply. She turned on the stereo and he took her in his arms and they swayed slowly to the music.

When she lisped, "I really like you a lot, honey," he drank up the warmth of her body and his mouth brushed her neck. Her flesh was firm with smooth, pointed breasts hard under the T-shirt. She wore no bra.

The music stopped and she went to the pillows and lay down on her back. He sat beside her and, bending down, kissed her softly on the lips. Trying to sound like David Niven, he said, "You know I want to make love to you, don't you?"

She sat up fast and said, "Just a minute and I'll freshen up and get into my nightie."

As she bounced into the bedroom, he thrilled to the idea of the ultimate conquest, to sexual enjoyment for its own sake.

Canby's words of five years ago came back to him then. "Selling is like seduction, Ted. The real future in this insurance game is in sales, but you've got to be aggressive and competitive. It's like seducing a woman. You've got to see it as a conquest. You're not the type, Ted. You're too conservative, too much like the old-fashioned guys with their twenty buttons on their gray flannel suit coats. There always have to be some peasants to do the clerical work if that's what you want but you'll never make any big money. That's why I'm leaving underwriting and going into sales." Canby had laughed and Ted had hated him ever since.

As he sat there in the squalid apartment, he thought about this girl who made him feel wanted and needed, and he needed her, too. Why didn't Alice ever need him? Need him for himself? Alice didn't seem to need anybody except their children.

Maybe it was his fault, and for the first time that evening he felt guilty. Had Alice ever been unfaithful to him? No, but he half wished she would have an affair sometime. Perhaps that would make her more exciting.

Even his guilt couldn't overcome his present feeling of smug satisfaction, of the sheer ecstasy of wrongdoing. He sat there, waiting and wondering if the girl suspected how old he was or did only he know about all the lifetimes that separated this woman–child from himself? Did she even care?

How could she know he was Don Quixote ready to joust windmills for her? With his heart full of unbearable loneliness, how tragic she hadn't the ability to understand all his needs, but Alice didn't understand them, either.

It occurred to him the girl had been gone a long time, but he thought it best not to call out and so he quietly walked into the bedroom.

She sat before the dresser mirror fussing with her lips and wearing only a shortie nightgown and bikini panties. Her legs and shoulders were tanned. He hoped she was tan all over. He stood in the doorway and said, "I must say you do look like Dulcinea,"

The girl looked puzzled. "Who?"

He smiled wistfully. "Nobody you've ever met."

This girl was no loose–morale hippie, he told himself. She was a beautiful princess, or an untouchable Playboy bunny. And all things, even love–making, had to be done properly because he was Don Quixote, Casanova, Don Juan, and Cyrano de Bergerac.

Quivering at the sight of her animal beauty, he felt weak. Glancing at him occasionally from her mirror, she made him feel as though this was his first time. How could he pretend to be a man of the world when he felt like a virgin? What if he was impotent?

As the girl sat before the mirror dabbing on eye makeup, he put his hands on her shoulders, turned her gently and kissed her again on the lips, sliding his tongue between her parted teeth.

She suggested they drink more wine. He filled the flutes from a fresh bottle he had brought into the room. Again, they drank deeply and after that, she went to the bed and lay down. Ted slipped off his shoes and shirt, sat on the bed, and wondered how to begin.

Perhaps Alice was right. Maybe he was just a little boy and maybe Canby was justified in calling him "old–fashioned" and "conservative." But Canby was a filthy–mouthed pig egomaniac who had the indecent effrontery to suggest the two of them swap wives some weekend.

With lust rising in him, he swept away the hair, pulled her head back and kissed her neck. He reached to unfasten her top when an insistent knock came at the front door.

This time he jumped up. She rose from the bed, moved through the living room to the door as he thought about his mounting excitement. The feeling was delicious—the unhurried chase, the sustained thrill.

Alice's idea of a thrilling time was to have her phony friends in on a Saturday night for a game of charades. All those dull house parties with all that silly chatter. What bores those people were! Why couldn't adult people sit down together anymore and talk about things that mattered?

He heard muttered whisperings at the door and the girl returned, murmuring something about maybe having to leave for a while to go across town to get something. Get what? Drugs? Was she a junkie?

She lay back down on the bed while he closed the venetian blinds and turned off the lamp on the nightstand.

Methodically, gently, he kissed her eyes and earlobes, stroked her hair, and massaged her shoulders.

Another knock came at the door! Still in her panties and shortie top, she went to answer it. He rose and followed her to the bedroom door, standing behind it so that he could see but not be seen. He watched her open the door a crack. He couldn't see the caller but he knew from the deep frantic whisperings that passed between the two of them that the caller was a man.

As she went out, he glimpsed a bearded face. Then she closed the door behind herself. He heard footsteps down the hall, the clump of heavy shoes and then the padding of bare feet.

Can this be happening he asked himself, determined not to lose control and spoil the magic. For the second time that evening, he found himself–sitting alone waiting in the darkness of that living room.

He picked up the bottle of wine and drank from it, ignoring the empty flutes. He emptied the bottle, went to the fridge for another one and went to the bathroom to urinate. An eternity passed before he finally accepted the fact that she was gone from his life forever. And he hadn't even asked her name. It could have been anything but Dulcinea.

Feeling cold, he went back into the bedroom and put on his shirt and shoes. Then, he stepped out on the balcony and looked down on the alley below, still clutching the bottle.

He thought about the destructive routine of his job, a highway to nowhere just like Canby said it would be. Canby was now a second vice president and netted over eighty grand a year. Why? Because Canby was a shrewd schemer with gall and drive who was corrupt enough to play politics while also playing golf with the company president.

Then Theodore J. Purvis, without really thinking, put his feet up and over the balcony railing. The balcony wasn't high enough–two stories above garbage cans and a pile of old lumber. The fall might not kill him, only cripple him for life.

He saw someone standing in the shadows below. A male voice called up to him. "Hey, you up there! Come down here a minute."

He withdrew his legs, crossed the living room and left the apartment, closing the door as he went. He stumbled down the two flights of dingy stairs and out into the alley to the voice that had called to him.

A youth stepped out of the dark. Ted saw at once another bearded face, ragged clothes, torn sandals, the grimy hands that had been rummaging in trash cans.

"Hey, man, that girl you were with tonight came running out like the place was on fire. She sure wasn't wearing much." He imitated her shivering, "This dude was waiting for her. Him and her ran across the street and jumped into a car that was waiting for them. It was packed with a bunch of people. They peeled out fast, like the pigs might have been after them. Hell, man, why'd you want to jump? These chicks are crazy! I mean they are nuts! You're better off without that one."

The kid raised his hand in the sign and said, "Peace, brother."

Ted said, "Peace to you too, kid," and took a deep swallow of wine. Then he handed the bottle to the bearded youth who took a long chug–a–lug and offered the bottle back. Ted shook his head. "Keep it, kid, and thanks."

Saturday was gray and dawning when he pulled into his driveway. The porch–light and living room light were on. Alice must have waited up for him. Once more, he felt the sting of guilt but she probably was sound asleep now and didn't hear the sound of his key in the lock or the front door opening.

But before he fell into exhausted slumber, Theodore J. Purvis knew he wasn't going anywhere. He was already there.

The Watermelon Dream

I told 'em my name was Bobby J. Carver and I didn't want no Big Buddy Pal. I told 'em I was nine years old and didn't need no Big Buddy Pal. I told 'em I had friends of my own and could take care of myself.

That's what I yelled at all those big ol' dudes sittin' around that table wearin' those suits and neckties all smilin' and tellin' me I was a "good little guy."

They was tryin' to get me to answer all kinds of questions about Lydia. Now Lydia ain't my mother or my stepmother or grandmother or foster mom or even related to me. She was my mother's friend and I been stayin' with her long as I can remember. I don't need nobody else.

Lydia had told me my real folks was killed in a car accident when I was a baby and I never had no brothers or sisters but I always got along okay.

Still, I'm kind of upset 'cause some friend of Lydia's talked her into sendin' me into this office place.

Anyway, 'there I sat with all those guys crowdin' around like a bunch or gays tryin' to shake my hand and squeezin' my shoulders with their fat white fingers.

The heavy one with the white hair and glasses who must have been the head cat looked me in the eyes and asked, "Do you like to go camping, hiking, and fishing, Bobby?"

Now those things sounded like fun but I figured there was some trick to it so I answered real careful like sayin', "Sure, they're okay, I guess, but I really prefer basketball."

The Cat guy went on to explain that these guys all belonged to some group named Big Buddy Pals Ink and they was supposed to help little kids and orphans and people like that what didn't have nobody to have fun with.

Well, I told 'em again for the hundredth time I didn't need nobody else 'cause I had Lydia so I wasn't really a orphan but they just kept smilin' and askin' questions about school and how I spent my time and what Lydia did for a livin' and all like that.

When they found out Lydia's husband had run off somewhere and wasn't livin' with us, they got real nosy. I was gettin' sick of those questions about Lydia 'cause she had always been real good to me and fixed me great things to eat so I kept still.

The Big Buddy Pals Ink finally let me go but two weeks later I had to go back down with Lydia to that big ol' office in Oakland again and she had to answer some questions and fill out about a trillion papers.

When that was over they told us there was some guy waitin' outside to meet us. They said he was goin' to be my Big Buddy Pal and I was to be his friend. I had to promise to do everythin' he said 'cause he was grown up and I wasn't.

The fat guy then goes outside awhile and pretty quick comes back in with this scared-lookin' guy he calls Glen. I have to shake Glen's cold hand and tell him my name and he looks kind of funny and I catch him takin' a peek at his palm as if he thinks maybe some black rubbed off on it or it's dirty or somethin'.

I pretend not to notice but I see this Glen guy with his fish eyes peerin' at Lydia behind his thick glasses but I really don't blame him for starin' 'cause Lydia is so pretty and sure smells good and her hair is all shiny and everthin'.

I always thought she looked a little like a combination of Tina Turner, Halle Berry, and that Bassett lady all rolled into one.

Lydia just acts cool, though, like she don't see nothin' and keeps talkin' to the fat guy.

About the time I think I can't stand all this crap any longer, they let me and Lydia go and I'm glad 'cause I'm hungry.

And bein' hungry makes me think again of the Watermelon Dream.

I'd had the dream before, many times. And it's always the same. There I am at this big ol' picnic and it's summer with me runnin around barefoot in the grass and swimmin' nekked. The mud is oozin' between my toes as I'm wadin' into that water. And after I've done swum and dived until I can't hardly get my breath any longer, comes time to eat. And Lydia and I and my brothers and sisters which I ain't never had sit down with some man who ain't got a face and we dig into those platters of sweet potatoes, okra, fried chicken, black-eyed peas, and watermelon. Oh, how I see the big and juicy melons with those black seeds sticking out just made for spittin'. About then, somebody coughs and I wake from the Watermelon Dream.

Glen kind of gives me a passin' glance and says he'll be seein' me soon and disappears through a side door after he shakes my hand and gives me sort of a hug and a pat on the ass. I wonder if he's just another of those fruity guys who get their fun squeezin' shoulders and pattin' butts. But Lydia smiles at me and whispers he ain't no Catholic priest.

One night about a week later, Lydia calls me into the kitchen and tells me this Glen guy is on the phone and wants to talk to me.

I pick up the phone and ol' Glen starts tellin' me he's got some free time and would I like to go on a campin' trip.

Right away I think back on how those big shots from Big Buddy Pals Ink asked me if I liked campin', and fishin' and stuff like that. At the time I thought they were tryin' to set it up so I could do those things by myself but now I see they plan on me doin' chis stuff with this Glen dude.

Since I can't think of an excuse real fast, I tell Glen okay and he tells me to be ready and he'll pick me up on Saturday mornin'.

Well, I forgot about the whole thing because when the next Friday rolls around, Lydia has one of her man friends in and we stay up real late watchin' TV and eatin' popcorn and it's about two in the morning before I go to my room, pooped out but happy.

I'm hardly asleep before the doorbell rings and Lydia goes down to answer it. There's ol' Glen and he's dressed up in outdoor–type clothes and he asks me if I'm ready for the campin' trip.

While Lydia gets him a cup or coffee, I hurry around to get into my jeans and tennis shoes. I had traded my fishin' pole for some comic books so I grab a bamboo stick I stole from a rug store and my big Buck foldin' hunter's knife.

All this time, I'm tryin' to be as quiet as I can because I don't want to wake up Lydia's man friend who's sleepin' on a fold–up bed in the upstairs hallway.

I creep downstairs and see Lydia and Glen starin' sleepily into each other's eyes as Lydia starts fixin' my breakfast.

As we leave, I see Glen smilin' at Lydia and I wonder what he'd say if he knew there was a guy named George Jones asleep upstairs.

I get into the front seat of Glen's car and we take off, wavin, at Lydia as we go. I look in the back and see all the fishin' poles and campin' stuff, and I begin to think maybe this might be fun after all.

We drive for about two thousand miles and I'm really tired and hungry when Glen pulls into a campground about noon.

Now Glen and I are both city guys and so by the time we get the car unloaded, learn how to set up the tent, build a fire and cook lunch, it's already late afternoon.

I figure it is time to try for some fish so Glen and I go down to this stream and I can see right away that he hadn't done much fishin'. Neither had I but I knew I could fake it which he couldn't.

I'll never forget the look on his race when he reached into the bait box for a worm. Seein' how chicken he was, I told him that since he was older, that I'd be the hook baiter.

I got to admit I was excited when I hooked into this big ol' fish 'cause I'd never caught a fish before. Ol' Glen is excited too, and he yanks a net off his waist and gets it under that trout and we bring it in. What is really amazin' is that I found out later we should have been usin' salmon eggs.

Anyway, ol' Glen keeps fishin' after that but he never does catch a fish. He keeps gettin' his line caught in the weeds and I feel sorry for him in his pale skin and glasses with all that fancy equipment.

All this time I'm fishin' from the bank but Glen's out in the middle in his fishin' vest and those big ol' 'flatable waders.

He gives up on the worms and he's usin' floatin' fly line with fake flies and all kinds of phony, sick–lookin' doodads and castin' way out. No fish would bite on that stuff.

Glen's got on one of those fishin' hats with about a million flies stickin' onto it. Ever'time I look at him I feel like sprayin' him with insect goop.

After awhile, he drags himself ashore where he gets his breath back and says there's no more fish in this stream so let's go on a hike.

I roll down my' jeans and put my tennies back on and he puts all his gear back in the tackle box. It must have weighed a ton but he don't seem to mind. I carry the fish and we go back to camp.

We start out walkin' on this trail and pretty quick I see the edge of a lake between the trees. So does Glen and he starts runnin' saying that now we'll have some good fishin' and maybe catch one of those rare Piute trouts. On the way, he stumbles and twists his ankle.

Then Glen starts talkin' about the same things he's been talking about all day He tells me how important it is I should be a good boy and a good American and do what Lydia tells me. He says it's wrong to steal, hate people, start riots and use drugs and alcohol. He says it ain't a perfect world but we got to try to improve it.

He talks about how important love is. He says that there's different kinds of love but they're all good whether a man loves God or Jesus, his brothers and sisters, a woman or even some pet animal.

He says he don't expect me to know much about lovin' a woman yet. He's kinda blushin when he's tellin' me this. Then he goes on to say how people in the same family should love each other a lot because someday they might not have each other anymore. I figure he's talkin' about my folks 'cause he ain't lookin' at me when he's sayin' this and his voice is kinda shaky.

By this time, I see he's rested enough and I tell ol' Glen let's start back so we do. It's startin' to get dark and by the time I show Glen where the camp is, been lost goin' in circles on about three different trails for about a hunnert hours.

I'm pretty tired before I get a fire goin' and heat some water and he helps me get supper and it's not bad except for the biscuits he burned but I eat 'em anyway.

It's really dark by now and Ol' Glen is sittin' close to the fire just sort of dreamin' into it. He tells me to check out the tent, unroll the sleepin' bags and see there are no snakes around. I ain't scared of snakes but I know Glen is so I do what he tells me.

After awhile, I come out of the tent and sort of sneak up behind Glen like I was playin' Indian and I plan to jump on his back like I saw Indians do to soldiers in the movies.

As I get closer, I notice Glen has got his billfold open on his lap. In the flickerin' firelight, I can see he's lookin' at photographs of some woman and a couple little kids.

About then he hears me and bends down quick hidin' the lures and tryin' to look like he don't have nothin' to hide. When turns around I can see his eyes are wet and I ask him if his ankle is hurtin' him but he says no the smoke just got in his eyes.

We go to bed and he tells me this bedtime story which I figure was wrote for three-year old kids but I listen and don't say nothin, to hurt his feelins'.

Glen lights a candle and then he asks me if I say prayers and I say I ain't never said prayers so he teaches me the one about lying down by still waters. When we finish that, we sit awhile in the candledark just swattin' at the mosquitos.

Finally, he blows out the candle and then ol' Glen just as natural like bends over and kisses my cheek!

Now I ain't never been kissed much 'cept by Lydia and I ain't never been kissed by any man before let alone a white man so I'm just struck dumb and cover my head up and pretend I'm asleep.

Nothin' much happens in the mornin' 'cause Glen sleeps till about noon and when he does get up I tell him I already fixed my breakfast so he don't have to bother. The truth is, I had a cold breakfast 'cause I can't stand any more of his cookin'.

He finally gets up and he's lost his glasses so he goes back in the tent to look for 'em. He finds them right under his foot as he steps inside and I hear the crunch.

I tell him that he looks cool with those cracked lens and bent frames so he wears 'em as if nothin' had happened.

I say let's go fishin' and he says okay and we try the stream again. Right away, ol' Glen hooks this ol' tire and he really sweats gettin' his line loose. About hunnert casts from then, though, Glen catches this little bitty fish.

He's jumping up and down all excited, sayin' he's going to have it put over his fireplace 'cause it's a rare Piute trout which he had been talkin' about yesterday.

Glen says it's time to start back so we load up the car and before long he's on the wrong road and we cross about a million bridges and it's gettin' late afternoon.

I start fidgetin' around and tell Glen I have to go pee and to pull in at the next gas station. I figure he's about out of gas anyway and a blindin' rain has started. I notice the windshield wipers don't work.

Finally, we pull into this ol' one pumper. It's got to be the world's worst gas station 'cause the guy says the only gas he has is in a can out back. While Glen is takin' care of the car I sneak around and find me an old roadmap so I can find out where we are.

I get it worked out and tell Glen which way to go 'cause neither of us can understand the gas station man's directions 'cause he's from Alabama and don't talk English anyway.

We get stuck in the mud a few times and that watery gas is makin' the car choke and wheeze but by the time it's dark, we pull into my driveway and Lydia comes to the door, lookin' all worried. Ol' Glen is cool and says he's sorry we're late.

He tells Lydia I had a great time and learned a lot about the outdoors but he don't go into what really happened.

Well, ol' Glen shakes my hand and gives me a shoulder hug and Lydia tells me to go upstairs, take a bath and put on my pajamas.

I start for the stairs and I look back and see ol' Glen and Lydia real close to each other holdin' hands.

It looks kind or strange seein' her little black hand in his white one but it makes me feel kinda warm inside. Maybe that's 'cause I'd seen lots or black men with white ladies before but never a black lady with a white man.

Pretty quick he's got his arms around her and they kiss each other and I don't look no more 'cause I feel like some honky Peepin' Tom.

So I crawl into bed and as soon as I'm asleep, you guessed it, I start havin' the Watermelon Dream and it's great 'cause this time it's in color. Also, Lydia and Glen are in it and Lydia's in a wedding dress with ol' Glen by her side.

About two weeks go by and we get another call from ol' Glen and this time he's got an idea I should go on a bicycle trip with him.

Thinkin' of all the problems I had on the campin' trip, I say why don't he just drop by and see me and Lydia instead. Especially since it's rainin'.

Ol' Glen hotfoots it across town in record time and the doorbell is ringin' just as the first batch of popcorn is done.

I got to admit I feel good seein' him come in and look at me like I'm a real human bein' and not just another black punk. His eyes is warm and twinkly when he hugs me and Lydia and I know my Watermelon Dream is comin' true more every minute.

Homer's Lament

My name is Homer P. Winslow and I'm bustin' to tell decent folks about something that happened to me once in this here Golden Bar State of Californy.

Now I ain't had much edumacation but I got religion and that's the truth. I don't reckon I missed church–goin' once since I come down here from Curley, Idaho, and that's been quite a spell now. Fer fact, I left Idaho on my sixteenth birthday three years ago.

Anyhow, I live out here on this big ol' ranch hospital home place. They got me takin' care of the lawns, plants, and trees 'cause I really know how to do that stuff. I'm sort of a gardener and caretaker of the home. That's what it is, a home.

Leastways, that's what Mr. Aldous B. Smythe calls it and he's the big boss over a whole passel of us including a foreman, a truck–fixer, and two guys who do nailin' and sawin' and work on the heatin' and air conditionin'.

A bunch or other folks live here, too, but they are kept inside most of the time. There are other people in white uniforms watchin' 'em so they won't wander off. That's 'cause they are sick in their heads and waitin' to get their brains worked on.

I like the job fine but don't hardly get into town 'cause I got so much work to do. Like all last winter when I spent my time pullin' slumps and diggin' ditches and other back–breakin' work.

Even though I get tared, I don't have no complaints 'cause I take a lot or pride in what I am specially since Tom Sly, who is the foreman, talked to us that night in the bunkhouse.

Last November, fer fact, he said, "Say Homer, you sure are lucky, bein' a gardener, 'cause gardeners arc really special people. After all, don't you know that Lady Chatterly's lover was a combination game–keeper, caretaker, and gardener?" All the guys are laughin' after he says that and I'm really rattled 'cause I don't know who Lady Chatterly is.

When they tell me she ain't no real lady but a storybook lady, I laugh as hard as the rest of 'em. Course, I ain't read much but I guess they're talkin' about some dirty story and I'm embarrassed. What I read is my mother's Bible. Especially since she and pa done got kilt in that earth dam what busted up in that Teton country.

Well, about the middle of January I start havin' these pains in my back and I know it's just muscle strain from all that liftin' and whatnot. I tell Mr. Smythe and he says what I need is a good rub–down with Sloan's linament. He tells me that his wife couldn't do it because now she's got "arther–itis."

Seein' as I was havin' all these pains one of the guys says to Mr. Smythe one day: "Hey, since we got to get supplies and equipment anyway, why don't you send Homer in the pickup after it and let him get his back fixed at the same time?"

When Mr. Smythe mentioned "rubdown," right away I thought of old Mrs. Squires and the good rubdowns she used to give back in Curley when I was a kid. Boy, she gave the workin' men a real treatment! She was fat and jolly, those big, thick, hornrimmed glasses and she had muscley arms that looked like Popeye's arms. Fer fact, kids used to say when we saw her comin' down the street, "Hey, here comes old Popeyes!"

Well, Mr. Smythe says okay and gives me a bunch of written instructions about how I'm to go into town this Friday night in the pickup and get a hotel room and bring back the stuff Saturday afternoon. He says he'll give me one whole night off to myself to do whatever I want with it but says I better get my back worked on.

Now I said I don't get much time off, except on Sundays to go to church and I ain't no dummy so I'm hopin' maybe I can go to the movin' pitchur show while I'm in town and I'm purdy excited thinkin' about that.

That Friday I leave the ranch after sundown and head into the city, feelin' good except fer my back which is killin' me.

Around 8 O'clock, I pulls into the city right past a whole bunch of honky tonks. That foot-stompin' music I hear comin' out of those places is hard to resist but I know I got business elsewhere.

After drivin' around a whole bunch in lotsa directions, I finally find a place on a side street that's got this big sign over it which reads "MASSAGE" and I park right in front and climb out, all achin' and limpin'.

I go in and first off I stumble over a chair 'cause the insides is so dark. A girl sittin' at a desk asks me what can she do fer me. In the dim light of a couple red bulbs I see she's wearin' a big smile and a blouse cut so low I turn my face away.

Right away I tell her she better go put a sweater on 'cause the night is chilly and she might catch a chest cold if she don't cover up her chest.

Since I'm comin' right from work I'm kind of dirty and I can feel sand in my ragged beard but the other guys comin' out grinnin' and clean lookin' got ragged beards, too, so I don't think nothin' of it. I kinda wonder when I see some of 'em sort of wobbly and walkin' weak though, 'cause their backs shouldn't be hurtin' no more by now.

The girl asks me what kind of a massage I want and I explain I didn't know there was more than one kind but I got pains in my back which need to be rubbed down real deep to get at those way inside sore muscles I been usin' all winter.

She looks like she don't understand my drift but tells me she'll get me an attendant to see to it right away. In the meantime, she shows me this big board which has got writ on it all the kinds of massages there is and the prices for each.

They got Swedish and Oriental and a lot of others which I don't savvy neither. Anyway, I pay her thirty bucks and say I'm here to get the works.

I go into a room and purdy quick a girl comes in and tells me her name is Vicki and she's my "technician." She's got real skinny arms and don't look at all like Mrs. Squires 'cause she's not wearin' much 'cept one of them rigs they call "halters" and a skirt which hits her way above the knees. I can see her belly button over it.

She tells me to take all my clothes off and hang 'em in the corner and she'll be right back. Now, this kind of bothers me 'cause Mrs. Squires only had the men take off their shirts but I do it anyway and put the towel that Vicki gave me around my waist.

Soon Vicki comes back in and tells me to go across the hall and take a hot shower and with lots of soap. I do that what she says and as I'm comin' out of the shower she meets me in the hall and tells me that now I have to take a sauna bath.

I don't even know what a sauna bath is but Vicki explains that it's just steam comin' off hot rocks which will make me feel good and wash out my skin real fine.

After about a half hour of sittin' in that sauna and sweatin' my brains out in that steam, I think I'm about done so get up to go out.

I find the door is locked and I'm being cooked alive. I see this little clock with numbers on it and the word "OFF", which is the way I turn the switch. The thing don't shut off and I finally figure the whole rig is timed but now broken and will turn off when it damn well wants to but I'm afraid I won't live that long so I start yellin' and bangin' on the door.

Purdy quick Vicki opens the door and bawls me out fer messin' with the switch. She says I got to take another shower which I do and it sure does feel good gettin' all that sweat off. By then, I feel twenty pounds lighter.

I go back across the hall and cool in the room I was first in and soon Vicki comes in and tells me to lay face down on the table. I do it and she starts getting a lot of lotions and bottles and powders around and starts rubbin' my legs.

I try to tell her my back is what hurts but she don't pay no never mind. She rubs my feet and toes, even between my toes.

Then she comes around to the other end of the table and tells me to relax as she starts rubbin' my hands, fingers, and arms. Soon she's workin' on my temples and eyeballs and I think this girl must be crazy to be workin' this hard, and on all the wrong places. She makes a pass or two at my neck with some sweet smellin' cream and douses me with talcum powder and after about twenty seconds, asks me if I'd like to turn over.

I really don't want to but I do turn over. Then, she removes her halter. Boy, Mrs. Squires sure wouldn't have done that!

Then, Vicki real quick snatches my towel and I'm lyin' there nekked! I try to pull the towel away from her, sayin' it ain't decent fer me to be layin' there nekked and helpless before a young girl. I tell her I'm a man now and not a boy anymore like I was with Mrs. Squires.

She don't listen and starts in rubbin' my chest and stomach. Then she goes around and starts on my legs and knees again. Her hands climb up my thighs and soon her fingers is brushin' my growin' part which I tell her to cut that out, ain't nice and I don't want to be responsible fer what I might do but she smiles and keeps right on rubbin'. She tickles me with her fingernails and it feels good but I'm scared and feelin' funny, trying to grab the towel or my clothes or somethin' to cover myself.

At last she stops ticklin', takes my right hand in hers and says, "Now, Homer, will you put my hand on any other part of your body you'd like massaged?" I try to put her hand on my back but she pulls it away, laughs out loud and squirts a bunch of creamy lotion on her hands.

She leans over and with both her hands, reaches between my legs and grabs my private thing. She starts workin' it up and down until it is really big and hard. Then, she starts movin' toward it with her mouth open when the room starts to shake and I hear a rumblin' noise all around us.

Somebody is bangin' on the door and I know somethin' is wrong and so does Vicki 'cause she turns white-faced and runs out.

The lotions, powders, and bottles are fallin' off the shelves and I realize there's an earthquake goin' on. It's a big one, too, and I think maybe Californy might really break off into the ocean like some folks seem to think it will someday.

I almost fall off the table, pull on my socks, and after I get into my underwear, tug on my Levi's, jump into my boots, I whip into my shirt, scram down a corridor buttonin', zippin', and bucklin' out a back door along an alley stumblin' over a couple or crates and trash cans.

I take a left, run a few blocks over the cracked sidewalks until the shakin' stops and finally get up enough spunk to sneak back and get in the pickup. After spendin' the rest or the night in a motel outside town, I get the supplies the next day and drive back home.

Haven't been back since. I still ain't never got that rubdown I need and I sure got rubbed the wrong way in Californy. Guess I'll have to go to a doc in Nevada to get my back fixed.

A Prayer for Josie

On the day before Christmas the doctors led Eustis T. Franklin into a small blue room where they sat him down and told him his son had died.

That was four days ago. He scarcely remembered the funeral and the gloomy holiday spent with his in–laws. However, he could well recall that bleak day over a year ago when the doctor said Jamie had symptoms of sickle–cell anemia.

The boy was just twelve years old and his only child. There would be no other children. Now Eustis waited numbly in the county hospital where Josie, his wife, lay stricken with double pneumonia in the third floor intensive care unit.

A nurse took him to Josie's bedside and his wife whispered, "Eustis, you knew the chil' was ailin'. If you had prayed, maybe God woulda saved him. Now that he's gone, promise me you'll go to church. Not for my sake but for yours."

In this time of crisis, he forgot all the years of her domination and bossy nagging. He blotted from his mind the acid tongue of her mother and the disapproval of her sisters. He remembered only her years of sacrifice and toil working to support the family.

So it was with a sense of family bondage as well as guilt and remorse that drove Eustis to do Josie's bidding. Near the symbolic twelfth day after Christmas, while the bitter snows of January fell on the city, his black hand clutched at the massive door of the ancient church.

Shivering fingers found the handle and he pushed inside, moved down the aisle, and stopped before the altar. The reflected light of a passing automobile illuminated his face as he spoke.

"Are ya up there, God? I dunno who ya are or what ya are but if you're up there, please hear ol' Eustis 'cause I'm prayin' now!"

The curved pews stood empty and mute, the quavering voice echoing off them.

"I ain't nothin' but a poor black man an' I got no right in a church fine as this but I came 'cause of Josie. I ain't got religion like she has. Always figgered a man needed nothin' but hisself, but now…"

A choir might have been singing but the only sounds were the roaring of the wind and the scratching of elm branches against stained glass windows.

A canvas–covered organ stood off to one side and dead flowers sprawled over the sides of baskets sitting on stands in the corners.

"Please don't let Josie die. She's all I got. I know I ain't been much of a husban' lately specially when I got drunk and lost them food stamps shootin' craps… an' I'm sorry fer bad mouthin' that poleese man down by the river yestiddy."

Moonlight shone on his shabby frame and a tear ran from a bruised eye onto an unshaven cheek.

"An' I don' wanta seem greedy but if it ain't askin' too much I wonder if ya could somehow fix it so we could take up an' go someplace else someplace away from the floodin' river, an' the cold an' the stink, an' the… me and Josie get kinda discouraged sometimes."

Through trembling lips, the shaky voice remained intent.

"Ever since the boy died if it wun't fer lovin' her I'd be gone. I cain't get no job an' I'm tard of lookin' fer one. Folks don't take kinely to us on welfare. I'm goin' now an' thanks fer listenin' to this here ol' nigger. Amen."

The shaggy head lowered, and the voice trailed into a whisper. All was silent. Then two quivering feet groped their way back up the aisle.

Gnarled hands reached for the handle, the door creaked open, and he plodded out into the night.

When he entered the tenement hallway, the public phone on the wall was ringing insistently. Dread clutching his heart, he picked up the receiver.

Then his mouth spread into a smile as he heard the doctor's good news.

Roger's Trip

In a back bedroom of a small house in the suburbs, Roger slept soundly until a buzzing sound woke him and he beat the air frantically with both hands but the fly persisted in annoying him.

It was hot in the room and Roger threw the damp sheet off himself, rubbed his eyes and crawled out of bed. His body was wet from perspiration and he had a sour taste in his mouth.

The house was quiet inside but as he looked up and out a window, he started hearing sounds of birds chirping, people's voices, and automobile traffic. He smelled flowers and recently cut grass.

He struggled out of his T-shirt and slid out of his shorts. His skin felt cooler to his touch, the sweat evaporating off his body, making it easier to breathe and gain a respite from the oppressive heat. It was good to be all alone naked and he gazed momentarily fascinated by the sight of his own genitals.

Suddenly thirsty for a drink of water, he gazed forlornly at the bathroom sink, the bathtub faucet and a fishbowl on top of a vanity table. The faucets wouldn't turn on which greatly frustrated him.

Then he slipped through the house, out the back door and into the alley. A light breeze blew through his blond hair. A block from home, he met a smiling man in a uniform carrying a bagful or paper.

The man grinned at Roger trotting along and said, "Hey, good morning young man. What's your name? What's your hurry? Is your house on fire or is this a footrace?" Roger grinned back and continued running even faster.

The sun and the air felt good touching his nakedness. If only he could find a garden hose or someone sprinkling a lawn. He would ask them for a drink.

A lady passed him on the other side of the street and called to him, saying, "I see you're out for a jog. Where are you going?"

Roger zigzagged one more block across lawns and flower beds to avoid the hot pavement on his bare feet. He looked back when he heard someone running and coming up fast behind him. Perhaps the someone was bringing him a cool drink of water. Nevertheless, he kept running and soon realized that the someone was his mother and she seemed angry about something.

He ran faster but she caught him by the arm and spanked him lightly on his bottom five times which made him cry. He was confused because he loved his mother.

What did he do wrong? And he had been feeling so free and good. All he wanted was a drink of water. But then, Roger was only TWO years old!

Patterns in Paradise

It was twilight when Evelyn Kanaka walked along the beach off Kahuku Point and flung her plumeria lei into the surf.

She watched it float out, then come circling back to bob against the shore. Did she really think it would float away? Of course not! They always floated back in to tell the tourists they would return to Hawaii someday.

But she was an island girl. What did she care about mainlanders and why did she really want to believe those stupid old legends?

Many of them she had learned as a child while sitting on the lap of her one-hundred-year-old great-grandmother. Many of them had to do with spirits, nature, and the early days of whaling ships. Evelyn had thought she had seen those ghost ships herself and also the face or her great-grand-mother reflected behind her in the bathroom mirror. And recently she thought she saw the old lady in the crowds at the International Bazaar.

Angrily, she tore the orchid from above her left ear and threw it into an eddy, noticing the ever-widening circles it created. Life was like that she thought, and people are like the lei and the orchid, caught in a series of circles.

When she was a child, her mother had told her that all the good a person does for others will be returned in full someday. And her church and school teachers had compared this life of good deeds to rings of flowers or shells.

She believed in this pattern of circles now more than ever on the eve other nineteenth birthday because she knew that all the bad things a person did came back also. That must be true because everything in her life seemed to have gone wrong lately.

First, there was that fight with her boyfriend, Steve Onaka. The argument was one that had no simple answers and they had reached a stalemate.

He had said, "Evelyn, you can stay here if you want and be a slave to the malihinis for the rest of your life but not me. I'm leaving. I don't know where I'm going but someplace where I have a chance at a future. If you love me, you'll come along. Also, you know our parents don't approve of our relationship.

She had thought about her mother who was also born here and her father who was working for the U.S. Navy when the Japanese bombed Pearl Harbor.

And here Steve, her Japanese–American friend, planning to take his five-foot, four-inch frame somewhere and become an empire builder. How strange life was! How ironic the cycles of human history!

Steve had continued, saying, "Are you really that proud of these chunks of lava? You mean to tell me you like these low wages, this servitude? Look at you! Graduated from high school and the best job you can get is as a clerk at the Ala Moana. You're asking me to believe you're going to be happy selling those goods to the tourists for the rest of your life?"

She had started to protest but he had said, "Are you going to put on that bunny suit over at the Liberty House and pass out candy to the kiddies on Easter from now 'til you're sixty-two and retired? And they call this paradise! Can't you see it's all a facade? All you have to do it go down along Hotel Street to see what's happening to these islands. And all those haoles coming over here trying to exploit us and adding to the ugliness. I don't know about you but I stare out across that water and feel trapped here. This place has grown too small, at least for me."

Evelyn smiled when she considered his small stature but inwardly smoldered with rage at his words, knowing he might be right. Her mother had told her of the long battles in the legislature. Finally, after all the arguments had been presented, Hawaii was granted statehood in the summer of 1959. Her mother had said the school bells had rung all day and there were bands and parades but the islanders had laughed and cried with mixed emotions knowing even then their culture was threatened.

Many of them knew the old ways would slowly disappear. The language would be lost. The poor would suffer and the welfare rolls increase. There would be more people and fewer jobs. The big monopolies would move in and destroy much of the natural beauty like that big American industrialist who wanted to build an amusement park on Waikiki Beach with a roller coaster and an artificial volcano that would erupt every half hour.

Evelyn had sometimes thought about the social problems of modern Hawaii—juvenile delinquency, unwed mothers, and encroaching bureaucracy. Many of her friends were finding it difficult to cope in this changing society.

Was this why she got started with drugs or down deep inside did she agree with Steve? Was she imprisoned here, impaled like a butterfly in a universal insect collection?

That painful conversation was five weeks ago and she and Steve had angrily broken off their relationship. Even though it was just a difference of opinion, she vowed he'd never touch her again.

Because of her rage and to make Steve jealous, she went out the following night with Steve's friend, Jeff Shimoda for a moonlight swim here on the Point. After the luau and the rum, Jeff had playfully kissed her and before she could control the situation, it had gone too far. She knew it wasn't all his fault.

A week or so later Evelyn felt the irritation and noticed the ugly discharges. The doctor at the clinic told her it was gonorrhea and wanted to know all her sexual contacts. She had to name Steve and Jeff and explain the details of the entire disgusting business.

So that, too, was a circle. Even venereal disease—the price she had to pay for her sin. Or was she just too generous with her favors? She had never thought of herself as promiscuous so what made her do it? Was it really just out of spite? Was it a need to be loved? Or was it something else, a wild irresistible call deep within her, a return to the primitive early days?

Evelyn thought again of her great-grandmother and the legends, the stories about the friendly young island girls who swam out to the whaling ships and climbed up the mooring ropes into the eager arms of stalwart white sailors.

As she stood on the hard, black sand, tears welled into her eyes as she looked out to sea and thought about her life. She loved the islands. They were her home. She belonged here. Why did it have to change? Why were they trying to kill her culture? She reached into her handbag and hesitated only momentarily before swallowing the tiny pill.

She looked again at the orchid she had thrown into the ocean. It was lying limp and lifeless in a tide pool and the circles were gone.

The blossom was from the plant Steve had given her. She had promised him she'd wear it until it wilted and then press it into her diary. Now it was over. Nothing would again be the same between them.

Far out beyond the breakwater, her wet eyes saw the ship. Awed and with shocked disbelief, she gazed at the ancient two-masted whaler. It looked just like the ones her great-grandmother had described.

Unable to control her emotions or her actions, she slipped off her puka shell necklace, earrings, muu-muu, sandals, everything, and stood nude there in the gathering darkness.

With a slow smile and staring, glassy eyed, she swam out to the whaler which seemed to be getting farther away. At last she drew alongside but where were the anchor ropes? Where were the smiling sailors? She paddled around the ship three more times before it disappeared in the mist. Soon she became exhausted and started back, finding it difficult to breathe. She looked once more at the distant land before lying back and slipping beneath the huge waves.

EARLY NEXT MORNING A BEACH maintenance crew found a naked human female body floating face down and lodged against a cluster of lava outcroppings off Kahuku Point.

The body was that of a white–haired, withered Hawaiian woman estimated by the coroner to be well over one–hundred years old. On the wrinkled left thigh was a small tattooed butterfly under the initials "E.K."

Francis with an "I"

Francis sat in his living room and waited, bracing himself for the upcoming ordeal, thinking about his perilous predicament and the strange vagaries of humans and the way history always seemed to repeat itself.

Over thirty–six years had passed since the Revolution and now those nasty British were at it again. Mankind never seemed to learn from its mistakes, he thought.

This mistake was called the War of 1812 but what was the difference? Wars were fought for economic and political reasons. It was all so redundant but innocent people died nevertheless.

However, he didn't see himself as innocent or noble. Rather, he felt guilty because his motive was purely economics. In fact, it was the reason he had agreed to bargain with the British and trade himself for one of their American prisoners, along with some extra loot. Officials and militia would be by within the hour to administer the exchange.

Francis knew the prisoner well, a certain Percival Watley, who Francis had once represented in court. Watley already owed him money in retainers and Francis knew that if Watley died in one of those filthy British prisons he, Francis, would never see his due.

Francis had defended Watley through a series of civil actions and this most recent one had been one of those messy, drawn–out cases involving property settlement. Yes, it had been a legal nightmare but Francis had fought hard for Watley and won.

At the appointed hour, a knock came at his door and he opened it to see three burly guards and two officers standing on his threshold.

Surrounded by the five red-coated men, he was marched down the street toward the harbor. He glanced back at the monogram on his house, the large gold letters "FSK" barely visible in the half-light of an anemic moon. He wondered if he would ever see his home again.

Night was almost over. The first streaks or dawn broke in the east. Was this the way it would end for him, he wondered. Was the last member of a proud family of attorneys destined to rot in some prison?

Though he loved his family, he had never liked the name his parents had given him. Francis! What kind of a name was that for a man? Why not George or Franklin? Was that part of the reason he had recently rebelled and given up his law practice to write poetry and songs?

Across the water, cannons boomed. Smoke billowed up from the small fires which surrounded Fort McHenry.

Prodding him along the pier, they finally threw him roughly into a longboat and rowed him out to a full-rigged sailing vessel anchored in the bay.

Once on deck, he looked out across the water and saw the American flag in all its glory even if now it was just a tattered remnant, torn shreds of red and white stripes, the white stars in a bullet-riddled field of blue.

As he watched the fort taking a terrible pounding, his heart swelled with pride and love for his country. Tears came to his eyes as he thought about the brave men dying down there. Could the regulars hold out until reinforcements arrived?

His captors flung him into an empty cabin and locked the door. Tearfully, he reached into his coat and brought out a few scraps of paper, a quill, and a bottle of ink.

He leaned back against the bulkhead and wrote, "Oh, say can I see…" He scratched out the "I" and wrote "you" and continued. "By the dawn's early light. What so proudly we hailed at the twilight's last gleaming. "He skipped a space and wrote, "The rocket's red glare, the bombs bursting in air…"

Those damn British, he thought. It's a good thing that most of their bombs are bursting in the air and not on the ground where they might kill civilians.

He heard a sound at the door, and an officer entered and said, "Well, patriot, we've already sent Watley ashore. We'll be sailing for England on the morning tide but first I have some questions. Just who exactly are you?"

"My name is Francis, sir. That's with an "is" on the end. The ladies spell theirs with an "es" on the end." Lord, how he hated that name.

Then the officer bellowed, "Don't mince words with mc. I want your full name and occupation. You must be either drunk or crazy or both."

Francis raised his head and spoke clearly. "My name is Francis Scott Key, sir. I'm a songwriter and a poet. Until recently I worked as an attorney."

"Don't take me for a fool. You must plan on spying on us or sabotaging this ship. What other reasons could you have? Why would you be fool enough to trade yourself for that stupid Watley?" the officer demanded.

Francis stubbornly refused to answer the questions, so guards were summoned. He was dragged between their beefy shoulders to starboard where he was shoved into a tiny brig. A guard was posted outside the door.

In the darkness, he saw a small window and moved toward it. Far below and across the water, the fight for McHenry was still raging. He brought out his paper and writing materials and started again.

"Whose bright stars and broad stripes," he wrote, "were so gallantly streaming"…

It was light now and he hadn't had anything to eat or drink for over twenty–four hours. Still, he forced himself to make an end to it even though he was dizzy and spots were swarming before his eyes.

He wrote, "Docs that star spangled banner yet wave, o'er the land of the free and the home of the brave?"

He quickly signed the crumpled paper, yet took care to sign it F. Scott Key. Why should he spell out that awful first name on this little verse which he supposed would be the last thing he would ever write?

Before the ink had dried, he heard the longshoremen shout, the hausers being loosened and the ship slowly sliding out of the harbor and into history.

Angela and Gloria

So I'm sitting here at my WP–510–word processor wondering how my life could have become so screwed up. It's hard to say just when everything started going wrong.

All I can do now is try to write it down the way it happened. Maybe I'll feel better if I do. Also, I would like to leave some kind of testimony and, hell, it's so unbelievable, nobody would buy the complete unadulterated fucked–up truth anyway.

It will read like some kind or pulp scientific fiction or a confession but it should really be an exposé. I just hope it doesn't fall into the hands of certain individuals who will try to sue me for defamation of character.

Anyway, I could be melodramatic and write that it is raining and there is a tap–tap–tapping on my chamber door as I'm typing and some black bird is chirping to quote the raven nevermore. But all that has been done before and so has all that bullshit about Lenore.

No, the sun is shining brightly and all I can think about is that bitch, Angela, not Lenore.

But I'm getting ahead of my story. That's a big fault in my prose, along with a lot of digression and not being able to separate the real from the unreal, the past from the present.

Anyway, I met Angela at some cocktail party and I thought we might have something going for us. We did seem to have some common interests and she was pretty, smart and witty but the fascinating thing was that her father was a big shot at Goodwear Tire and Rubber and I just happened to be a skilled chemist in rubber products.

I'll never forget the expression on her face when I explained I worked in Stamford, Connecticut for one of the world's largest manufacturers of rubber goods. Actually, I was a struggling not–so–young underpaid maker and tester of prophylactics. That's right, condoms. People used to call them "rubbers."

I had really given my all for the company and in four short years had brought the industry a long way from the first rubbers which were so thick and bulky that using one was like taking a shower with clothes on.

I had advanced the industry to gossamer–thin condoms in a variety of styles and colors with ribs and studs on them. Then, I made some fancy French ticklers and later came up with the idea of dry lubricants and that little tit which is really a semen reservoir. Of course, this was all before the HIV virus and the AIDS epidemic but condom sales were high even then.

After Angela's first shock at finding out what I did for a living, I know now she saw me as just some sort of amusing lapdog, not very much different from other men she'd known. I think she got her rocks off explaining to her girlfriends the juicy details of my job.

However, I fancied myself in love with her and she did have personality, sense of humor, charm, beauty, and intelligence. What else is there? To me, she seemed perfect, everybody's dream girl as well as the natural girl–next–door type. She could be a tomboy or terribly sophisticated. She was as changeable as the weather: unpredictable and challenging.

After the usual candy, flowers, and candlelight dinners as well as a few loving gifts of jewelry, lace undies and baby–doll nightgowns, we became engaged.

Now it's strange, looking back, that I couldn't see her for what she really was, a spoiled brat, a terribly immature child so incredibly emasculating, aggressive, and ambitious that she just used me as her boy–toy, a special dildo. She had about as much sensitivity to my needs as a streetwalker.

Any guys reading this that think it's smart to marry the boss's daughter or be the son the boss never had forget it. From my experience, those things may happen in novels and movies but not in real life. But I'm getting ahead or my story again.

Anyway, like a fool I let her talk me into going to work for the Goodwear people and, of course, her father got me the job. I should have known better because I didn't like him from the first time I met him in his Danish–modern office with Angela sitting there trying to look so wise with her legs crossed and wearing that terrific hairdo.

That bitch, sweet and innocent on the outside but inside a barracuda obsessed with a Delilah complex. I should have suspected that when we were in bed together and she insisted on getting on top and riding me like I was a gelding in the Santa Anita Handicap. And she always consummated quickly, just a few strokes to satisfy herself and then she pulled me out and jerked me off. Never even a blow–job from that fastidious cunt but of course she always wanted me to go down on her.

During the engagement period, she used every possible kind of birth control and even insisted on me using the finest products from my previous employer. I think she went out of her way not to see my semen because she'd jump up and run into the bathroom right after I climaxed. It's a wonder she never asked me to get a vasectomy.

I know her father had no idea what kind of woman she really was and since her mother was dead, I think the old goat had forgotten about sex long ago. He was so stupid about life he probably thought Angela was a virgin and we spent our time together just holding hands.

I'm ashamed to admit it but the old bastard hired me for a salary that was just slightly more than I was getting from my former employer.

So I went from making condoms to making tires and in two fast years I was the head man turning out the famous Goodwear 500 radial tire. My colleagues in the lab started hanging nicknames on me like Rubber King, Goodfire, and even Goodwear Junior.

My paychecks saw substantial increases but then the reports started coming in about all the fatal accidents and some female writer in California was demanding an investigation. It seems a blown 500 radial tire caused an accident which nearly killed her and her kids on some freeway out of L.A. while she was driving her station wagon at 90–plus miles an hour across the Mojave Desert.

But that woman was right! There was something wrong with the Goodwear 500 tire. And I wanted to find out what it was even if I had to raise hell, call in Nader's Raiders and fire every incompetent sonofabitch who had anything to do with it.

But wouldn't you know it? That fucking old goat, Angela's father, fought the investigation as well as the press and tried to deny any responsibility whatsoever.

I went to the asshole and told him point blank that the continued production of the Goodwear 500 was tantamount to murder and I didn't want any part of it. He told me in no uncertain terms to forget it and go soak my head and that if I couldn't stand the heat to get the hell out of his kitchen.

My relationship became more and more strained with the Goodwear people and eventually I resigned before the old bastard could fire me. I knew I had to live with my conscience and I kept having nightmares about all those dead people and the blood and gore scattered along all those highways.

Naturally, this also meant my relationship with Angela was over as well as my job. I'm just thankful I didn't marry her and that we never had kids or she would have really wiped me out financially and taken custody of our children.

I retired to my lonely apartment and just sat for long hours staring out my picture window, horny as a goat with a choking erection. like somebody all dressed up with nowhere to go.

I felt like I never wanted anything to do with women again. I became a recluse and might as well have been a monk in some monastery or a guru on some mountaintop meditating my life away.

But I couldn't turn off the physical side of my being and masturbation became my way or life despite my experiments with meta-physics, holistic medicine, and even group therapy.

I found I could escape my problems somewhat by reading and, eventually, as the months went by, I turned from reading garbage to the classics. I kept up my physical strength with an ab roller, barbells and stationary jogging.

I should mention I had moved to Oakland, California, and had filed for Chapter 13. I was living on unemployment insurance and knew when that ran out, I would have to go on welfare and that meant only food stamps.

Not everybody knows that if you voluntarily quit a job like I did, it takes at least six weeks for the unemployment checks to start coming in. Many a time I went hungry waiting for them. Of course, they were delayed because I had come from another state.

I had gone from a $300,000-a-year job to bankruptcy, my savings were used up and some investments I'd made in the stock market went sour.

So I kept reading the classics and jerking off, trying to forget my misspent youth and the treacherous nature of the female sex. I could see I had become a woman-hater and knew that impotence was just a see a matter of time.

One night I became fascinated with Offenbach's light opera, "The Tales of Hoffmann," I was enchanted from the prologue describing Hoffmann drinking with friends in a Nuremberg tavern.

Then comes the first act which takes place in the home of the self-styled scientist and inventor, an Italian named Spalanzani. This is only one part of the many Tales of Hoffmann.

I could somehow relate to all this because this guy was supposed to have a remarkable daughter, the beautiful Olympia, who was actually a mechanical doll. I could see, as a scientist myself, the advantages of a home-made female, especially after my life with

Angela. Olympia, like Angela, was supposed to be the perfect woman who could, along with all her other talents, sing and dance divinely.

And then in comes Hoffmann for the coming-out party for young Olympia. With Hoffmann is his friend, Nicklausse, and the evil genius, Coppelius, who sells Hoffmann a pair of eyeglasses for the occasion. Through these glasses, Hoffmann, obviously as horny as I am, sees the robot as a vision of unsurpassing beauty.

Olympia sings to the delighted throng, and among others, goes straight to Hoffmann's heart. He declares his passion for her openly at the first opportunity and she responds in stuttering monosyllables.

In one scene, the lovestruck Hoffmann had finally shyly and impetuously taken Olympia's hand which sets a mechanism in motion and the girl rises from the divan, circles the room and seductively moves toward the bedroom with Hoffmann in excited pursuit.

She dances better than she talks and accepts Hoffmann as her dancing partner. Immediately I think of that bitch, Angela, again, because there wasn't a dance created that Angela couldn't do.

The two dance faster and raster until Hoffmann, middle-aged and pushing the hell out of fifty, can no longer keep up and falls exhausted on her ballet slippers.

She flits from the room and a crashing sound is heard. Coppelius returns with the mutilated figure of Olympia, the automaton, lying lifeless in his arms.

The doll had been constructed by Spalanzani and Coppelius, but Coppelius then claims that Spalanzani deceived him and now demands payment. The two quarrel while Hoffmann mourns for his lost love. As the scene ends, he cries out in bewilderment and despair. Oh, how I could relate to all this!

The scientist had explained that when wearing the glasses, one may look into the heart and soul of a woman. I thought this was just a bunch of bullshit but then I started rereading some of the passages. I thought about how marvelous a home-made doll would be.

I kept thinking how terrific it would have been if the special eye–glasses worth 500 ducats weren't necessary. Why not endow Olympia with all the desirable qualities of a woman and yet make her out of real flesh and blood?

I thought about this for weeks after my rereading and eventually said out loud to myself, "Shit, why not? I'm an inventor and a good chemist and this is the twenty–first century. I ought to be able to make a woman at least as good as Olympia. And I have all the modern–day natural and synthetic materials at my disposal."

I was familiar with the first crude inflatable dolls which were sold in dirty book stores to perverted men who were unable to relate to the opposite sex. As a lark, I had even made a few of them myself as a hobby while working at Stamford.

All this was akin to the old joke about that man named Dave who kept a dead whore in a cave. He said, "I'll admit I'm a bit of a shit but think of the money I'll save!"

And then I thought about the three guys and one woman on a desert island. The three guys were supposedly pretty ashamed of how they were treating her but couldn't stop themselves and eventually she got some venereal disease and died. Soon the three men were so ashamed of what they were doing to her, they buried her. Then they got so ashamed of what they were doing, they dug her up again.

Well, those two old rhubarb classic lousy jokes made me feel like I was going to puke but I kept reading and studying feverishly night and day thinking about the possibilities.

By that time, I was really impoverished and had sold most of my possessions for cheap wine which kept me in a stupor.

I had kept all my notes and formulas and knew everything there was to know about the nature of rubber and rubber products. I even delved into the mysteries of plastic and vinyl as well as all the fundamentals of puppetry, human anatomy, and biology.

Soon I had set up a small but efficient laboratory in my studio apartment, complete with test tubes, beakers, vulcanizers, and Bunson burners and started to do serious, hands–on work.

Still, poverty and hunger plagued me and I had no luck in getting any kind of job. About all I had left is this beat-up word processor, some ragged clothes and my chemicals and equipment. Soon, I'd be evicted and homeless.

Model after model turned out with some slight imperfection and even though I felt like a frustrated rapist and murderer, I simply couldn't seem to stop ravishing each one after plying them with wine and then stealthily creeping out each night to dispose of them in the incinerator.

After six months, the prototypes started to get better and the skin and muscle textures got more lifelike. The bodies were more like large Barbie dolls but the mechanical aspects still left much to be desired. Incredibly, way beyond my expectations, the robots were all very affectionate and had none of the nasty qualities I had found in Angela. They were gentle and non-aggressive, personable and happy.

However, they were all certainly a great improvement over masturbation and I know with my perverted sense of humor, that even old men in the back rooms of butcher shops throwing quick fucks into raw liver have nothing on my beauties. Actually, I should be grateful to those old men because they gave me the inspiration for my ultimate ideal.

But it was more than just the image of those men that triggered the inspiration. it was really an outgrowth of that trip I'd taken so long ago through Malaysia, Penang, and the whole of Indonesia to inspect rubber plantations for Goodwear.

The team would lay over at intervals in Singapore to regroup and take on supplies and it was there that the beauty of the Asian girls working in the banks and shops made an everlasting impression on me.

I decided my next and probably last attempt to make a humanoid would be Asian and Oriental in concept. She would have almond-shaped eyes, long thin legs, perfect facial features with high cheekbones and black hair.

She would be a combination of the Dragon Lady and Suzy Wong and I would outfit her in high heels, wine-red skirts slit up the side, earrings and kimonos. She would have the grace and charm of a Madame Butterfly, the warmth and gentleness of a Tahitian belle the personification of every wonderful Eurasian woman I'd ever met I would name her Gloria Chan.

That was two months ago and I have scrapped four models already. I just can't get them Asian enough or else there is some little flaw like a defective speech pattern.

I have just placed the fifth Gloria out by the dumpster because I couldn't bear to throw her in my poor–man's "crematorium." She is so beautiful and the only thing wrong with her is that I tried the stupid idea or binding her feet as they once did in ancient China. Now her feet are small but she can't walk.

So I just propped her up there against the dumpster and at the last minute decided to unbind her feet so when the trash men come she'll be more presentable. Also, I wouldn't want them to think I'm completely crazy and don't know the first thing about women. It would be like a guy working in a department store window and getting a mannequin's arms on backwards.

Not that it will make any difference, really. Well, I'm going back inside now after one last kiss from Gloria just slumped there crying. She'll be dead by morning because I've removed her transistors.

Now I'm sitting here at my work table in front of this sheet of paper struggling to write these last few words somehow. I have prepared a lethal injection and poured a final glass of wine. I'll also be dead by morning.

The twilight has gone and night shadows creep through the windows. A knock at the door. Who can that be at this hour? I rise from my chair and shout, "Who's there?" Nobody answers so now I'm reaching for the doorknob angrier than hell about being disturbed.

I open the door and see Gloria standing there gasping for breath. As she starts to collapse, I catch her in my arms, reach for the transistors in my lab coat and say, "Welcome back, Gloria. Come in my darling."

Dogwood Memory

Austin B. Briggs sat in his living room looking out at the birds pecking on the lawn, at the gently swaying blossoms on the tiny dogwood and again felt the lump in his throat, the tightening in his chest and the twinge that he knew wasn't from indigestion.

On warm spring days like this one he really sensed the loss of her. Damn it, he thought, maybe it would be better to scream it out loud once in a while, to express anguish and anger at the world rather than keep it locked inside. Not to verbalize it was to allow it to be a festering sore or to resemble some savage caged animal.

He knew his kids would be coming home from school hungry and he still had the laundry to do. Perhaps he should order pizza. He didn't feel like taking them out to eat, not on a school night. Maybe he could fix them some sandwiches or cold cuts, anything to prevent a lengthy cleanup.

Oh, God, why was life so hard, cruel, and demanding? And now all the meaning had gone out or it. Still, he knew it would be so much worse without the children and the dog and cat.

Sure, there had been all those friends who came at first, all those sympathizers, the counselors who were experts at handling the affairs of families under stress. And before them, all the relatives with their cloying pity. What good did it do except maybe to keep him from going insane? Maybe he was going insane anyway.

He heard the kids come in banging the door and rushing to their rooms. He had been strict at first and insisted on clean clothes, scrubbed hands and faces by suppertime and had subtly suggested to his precocious darlings that it might be wise to change clothes, clean up their rooms, and start their homework as soon as they got home afterschool. That way, they would have a jump on the good primetime television programs, he had said.

He looked again at the little dogwood. It would always be her tree and It was only a scraggly branch when she planted it. She had raised that tree almost as lovingly as she raised the kids. He smiled as he thought back, remembering how she had watered it so faithfully, fed it regularly and brushed the snow away from it in the winter so it wouldn't freeze.

When she first became ill in 1966, he thought he might remove it because it was so much bother but he knew he had no right to do that. It was her tree and more than that, now it was about all he had left to remember her by. Neither of them had ever been much for coveting material possessions such as antique furniture, precious stones, coins, or stamps.

Thinking back, he recalled his sadness the day of the yard sale when women came to go through her clothes and shoes. Did those women feel like pariahs or just look like them? Later, many of her things were either sold or given away to charities so there wasn't much left to remind him or their life together except the photo albums. And the tree.

And though he now loved the tree and had grown used to tending it in her absence, sometimes it served to give him a really bad case of the old moody blues. But lately, even worse than the blues was the guilt.

Guilt could be a terrible thing but looking at it objectively, he had no reason to keep flogging himself for something he couldn't have prevented. It was just that she was so all alone. Nobody should be alone when death arrives. It wasn't his fault he couldn't be there, but suppose she had wanted to tell him something or wanted him to do some little thing at her bedside.

Damn that disease! The one with that terrible unforgiving name, lupus erythematosus. Mostly, a woman's disease with no cure.

The kids came bounding down the stairs and Janie yelled, "Hey, Daddy, where's my white blouse? I've got to have it for that school party tonight. And don't forget you promised to drive me over to Jeff's house first."

Oh Lord, the demands, he thought. The demands were continuous, unending, and the rewards were nebulous, uncertain, perhaps even nonexistent. How long could he go on like this?

"Just a minute, honey. Let Daddy get organized. I think your blouse is hanging in the garage. Why don't you look there first? Then go and wash your hands and face and pour yourself a glass of milk. Hey, you guys want pizza, tonight?"

Then his thoughts drifted back, back to their early life together. They were deeply in love, just two kids, really. He couldn't keep his hands off her. She'd write little love notes and poems to him and hide them all over the house; in the closets, under his pillow and more than once, in his lunchbox. The guys really teased him about that.

There was the time she damaged the car and thought he'd be mad and it took her half the night to get up enough courage to tell him about it. He had felt like blowing his top but what the heck? What could he say? She hadn't been hurt and it was just a car, replaceable like almost everything else in life. Everything but her.

He remembered the family picnics in the park with their parents and little incidents like the time he came home early in the middle of the day and caught her crying over some sad and silly soap opera. Maybe it wasn't so silly and perhaps little happenings like that were not so little.

Even back before the beginning of her sickness, it had been hard to cope with the expense of a family and once they thought they might lose the house to foreclosure.

Then, after all the tests, they realized the disease was resisting medication, just a matter of time before she would be bedridden. There was even talk of sending the two girls to live in foster homes for awhile. But neither or them believed it could possibly get that bad that soon.

Then came that night he had had to leave town. When he got home, it was already too late. She was gone. And so that night in the early spring of 1983 when bluebirds sang and she was so all alone, the angels came. He liked to think that's what happened to her; the angels came and took her away to some pleasant place forever.

His youngest daughter, Brenda, came into the room at that moment and turned on the television set but seemed to not even see him sitting there.

He said, "Brenda, would you please feed Tiger and Bunny and make sure they have fresh water?"

"Aw, Daddy, do I have to? I'm really busy right now."

"Yes, you have to," he said, following her to the garage where the pets were waiting expectantly.

He glanced over at the washer and dryer and noticed that Janie had found her blouse. He rapidly sorted through the nearby clothes hamper, shoved a load into the washer, added soap and turned it on.

He went back into the house, sat down and thought again of the dogwood. He swung the recliner around to look out the picture window again, at the little tree and the yard that was like a stage where she sang and laughed and their love grew up. But without her the stage was somehow bare and he was just sitting there like some stupid baffled clown.

Now, when dark clouds passed overhead, they rained down on the flower beds and on that little tree she planted. It was thoughts like those that kept him faithful to her memory even though he knew he couldn't live the rest of his life alone.

And then in the din of television sounds in the background and with his daughters arguing between themselves over some trivial matter, he thought back about all her days in hospitals, all the many waiting rooms where he has sat and pondered their life together. And it was all those days of all those months of all those years that slowly eroded away their joy, and love just wasn't enough.

He recalled that day when the doctors came and sat him down in that small green room and told him his wife was going to die. They told him they had done all they could, that despite modern medical science and that team of fourteen specialists and all that experimentation with combinations of drugs, that she was on the way out. Here was one rare vicious disease that had whipped them all and its mark was to be that terrible butterfly rash on the bridge of her nose.

Oh, he had thought of leaving her, of just getting on a Greyhound bus or a plane and running off to some place in the sun far away.

His sister's husband had done that when his sister was diagnosed with multiple sclerosis. Yes, he could have ended the marriage and their relationship but not ended his personal agony if he had been that cowardly.

And as her condition had worsened, intimacy suffered and he cursed the fact he couldn't eliminate his own physical lust. He had thought of searching out some understanding friend who could give him the sexual healing he seemed to crave more each day. But that was adultery: immoral, impractical, and a lot or other bad things, too.

So he could never quite bring himself to do it, or even to sneak around behind her back and have some shabby affair with some promiscuous woman or prostitute on some back street where no one would ever know.

Then. there had been Lisa, that widow who lived a couple of blocks down. She had looked at him with her hot eyes at the church bazaar, and then had held him close while dancing in that not-so-long-ago. She had whispered, "Austin, make love to me" while chewing his earlobe.

No, there were no solutions to that problem because of the way he felt about open marriage and divorce. It was just that he knew down deep inside that it wasn't right to leave someone because they were sick. Two people married for better or worse and life was like that. Everybody starts out in life with a hand of cards and everybody plays them out as well as they can to the end. There are no guarantees.

He knew she wouldn't have left him if the situation had been reversed, if he had been the one with the incurable disease. It would have taken more than that for her not to love him.

They both had known other couples who parted for reasons of bad health and it was usually the man who couldn't cope with the idea of a terminal illness. The women were the strong ones.

THE HOUSE WAS DARK NOW. Shadows were moving in and the moon was rising. Jamie was back from her party and Brenda's television programs were over. Both girls were upstairs in their rooms, hopefully asleep. Outside, little night birds were flitting in the small dogwood tree.

Austin B. Briggs rose from his recliner and pulled the drapes over the picture window. He sat back down again and realized how unhappy he was, almost like his had been an unfulfilled life. But it was more than that and more than his loss of her.

He felt cheated and angry and he guessed it was all those many mixed feelings that kept him from committing suicide.

Lately, as he sat at his office desk downtown, he would look out the windows and dream of his free childhood and of sailing ships and airplanes and he just mostly wanted to go somewhere and live life like a real man.

He didn't know what that meant exactly but discovery, exploration and adventure were all a part of it and so was not ever again feeling lonely.

NEXT MORNING, HE AWOKE TO a beautiful and bright sunny day. For unknown reasons, he felt happy and confident.

He sat back in his recliner with his coffee cup in his hand waiting for his daughters to come running down the stairs. He thought about how proud he was of them. To him, they were perfect in every way, truly blessings from his marriage.

Feeling ashamed, guilty, and selfish about his thoughts of the previous evening and his dreams of starting a new life by himself, he squelched those thoughts and told himself he was really a lucky guy in many ways.

Out loud he said, "We are all in good health and when you've got your health, you've got just about everything. It was rough for awhile but we have this big house and enough money for food and other necessities. I have a great job with good chances for advancement. We have what really counts in life. I should try to help others, maybe even start going back to church. Who knows, I might meet some good woman and…"

He smiled as he started upstairs, met his daughters on the landing and yelled at them, "Yes, I'm a very lucky man."

Glancing out the patio door on the way down, it seemed to him that the little dogwood tree had grown two feet overnight.

PART TWO

MEMOIRS

Freedom Train Revisited

The 1976 version or the American Freedom Train has come and gone but for years I have wondered how I missed seeing the train when it passed through Spokane, Washington, in the late 1940s. The train carried copies of the historical documents related to the organization of, exploration, and settling of America such as the Declaration of Independence and the Constitution.

I remember standing in the long lines as a teenager but never getting inside to see the displays. Was it because it started to rain? Was it because they closed for lunch just as I got to the ticket window? Was the price so high I couldn't afford a ticket?

Recently, I determined to find the reason so I rummaged through the garage and found an old suitcase where I keep memories and came across a battered five-year diary.

It took me quite a while to find it but at last I found the entry of April 13, 1948, which read as follows: "Willie, Dave and I went with Bill Coe and his mother today to see the Freedom Train. We couldn't see it because of the crowds. Instead, we saw Macbeth, a road play."

There was the answer. Crowds. Even back then, there were crowds. Was I too impatient, tired or disgusted to wait or was it others in my group who couldn't stand the waiting?

At this writing, that was twenty-eight years ago and I didn't want to make the same mistake again so on another twenty-eighth, the twenty-eighth of November, 1975, when the Freedom Train stopped in Sacramento for a three-day layover, I was ready and eagerly waiting.

In fact, I drove down into Old Sacramento on Thanksgiving night to watch the technicians set up and to peek inside the locomotive. I even took my wife and kids and we got to peer through the windows of the coach cars at the lunar model used on the moon. Of course, they couldn't have had that displayed back in 1948!

I couldn't remember the ticket price back then but in 1975 the sign on the kiosk read two dollars for an adult ticket. I figured I could steal that much from the kids' piggy banks if 1 had to. However, I decided to splurge and take the whole family with me the next morning.

After all, I didn't want them to have the same burden of curiosity I'd carried with me all these years.

The 28th dawned cold, clear and crisp and, unable to find a nearby parking space, we ended up in Yolo County and had to walk back across the Tower Bridge.

It was about 10:30 a.m. and crawling humanity must have stretched as far as midtown, roped off and sectioned with yellow cords like some kind of a maze or an obstacle course for a bicycle race. All those people reminded me of cattle being driven into a loading chute.

I don't know what I expected but it was every bit the spectacle it was back in Spokane so long ago; however, maybe only society changes and not the patterns of history because it all seemed faintly, dreamily familiar.

There were the inevitable marching bands, the flags, displays of red, white and blue bunting, and the tents selling patriotic doo-dads. No doubt some of all this hoopla was designed to prepare us all for the coming bicentennial year.

And the people. All kinds, but mostly families. Fathers carrying their young in backpack carriers, a woman sitting on a curb breastfeeding her baby with her back to the biting north wind. Was that her husband or her boyfriend standing in the ticket line? In 1948, it would have been her husband.

A black man dressed in revolutionary garb strolled about looking not really like an officer from Washington's army. A band played "The Stars And Stripes Forever" while a mixed group of young singers and dancers looking as clean and wholesome as those on the Lawrence Welk Show performed nearby on a hastily erected stage.

Suddenly, I was proud to be an American and was duly impressed by all the patriotism being shown. Here were thousands waiting in orderly lines for two–and–a–half hours to see a little bit of America.

And after all that had happened since 1948! After Korea, after political assassinations, after Vietnam, after corrupt leadership and the Watergate scandal. After all this and more, apparently, people still loved their country enough to drive in for miles from surrounding towns to stand there and suffer the crowds and the cold out of that love alone.

I gazed around at the stands selling cotton candy, soft drinks, hats, personalized T–shirts and bicentennial mementos while behind us a young mother with a toddler named Randy were marking time to the stirring beat of a John Phillips Souza march.

Perhaps some would say it was all just a bid to bolster the economy, a tricky commercial venture to boost the bicentennial and sell gadgets and junk. After all, what kind of person would want an ash tray in his sophisticated <u>Better Homes And Gardens</u> house with the words, "I bought this at The American Freedom Train" printed on it?

There were a few line crashers but they were just young kids who hadn't lived much history. Rudeness transcends all of humankind and knows no national origins or historical epochs.

All races and nationalities were represented in the patient lines. The blacks, the Hispanics, even some Native Americans. There were many Asians, some of whom judging from their wide–eyed stares, were probably refugees recently out of Vietnam and Laos. There were also Chinese, Koreans and Japanese.

The old and the young, the–well–to–do and those of meager means, the babies in arms and in strollers, the disabled on crutches and in wheelchairs or with canes or walkers, all were there.

Finally, at 1 p.m., we moved up the boarding ramp and I looked down on the human sea. I felt like making a speech on patriotism and telling the crowd how proud I was of them but I didn't. I didn't even wave the way celebrities do when they wave at airports. I wasn't a celebrity. I just handed over my ticket and walked inside still not quite believing I was at last going in.

We stepped on a conveyor belt and watched America unfold from its origins through its inventions to its sports and arts and leaders. Bits and pieces of conversation from tape recorders caressed our ears while our eyes tried to take it all in, reading as fast as we could. That wasn't easy considering the length of the Constitution, the Declaration of Independence, the Emancipation Proclamation, the Monroe Doctrine, and the surrender papers of the Japanese in 1945.

In twenty–two minutes it was over and we stepped outside. We walked down another ramp and skirted the crowd out to what is now Front Street.

I looked across at the Old Eagle Theater. The marquee was blank. The doors were locked. It was now just another tourist attraction. No Mark Twain, no Lily Langtry, no Macbeth road play. Not even porn star Linda Lovelace. Sign of the times I suppose. Too bad. I really would have enjoyed seeing it again. Not Linda Lovelace. I mean Macbeth.

My Lost Love

She left me todays While I was at work. Not even a hasty farewell. Nothing. Gone without a trace. And I thought she loved me. Why would she do this to me?

It had been raining heavily and as thunder boomed, lightning flashes split jagged across the skies.

I loved her so much and had grown so accustomed to her ways, I wondered if 1 could live without her. I thought about her kind brown eyes with gentleness shining in them. I thought about all her feminine charms, the way she moved her bottom when she walked and her wet, sloppy kisses.

Then I panicked and called the neighbors, asking if they'd seen her. With aching heart, I got in my car and drove, just drove blindly in a foolish hope I'd see her walking along some wet street.

How I wished the rain would sweep her through the boulevards and wash her back upon my doorstep.

I thought about the large gap in my life her absence would leave, I felt it already.

Oh, she had her faults. Nobody's perfect. She wasn't petite, probably weighed 150 pounds, maybe more, and no amount of exercise could shrink her.

She was messy around the house but I had learned to live with that because she was like a loving, muscular slave born to do my bidding.

All she demanded from me was close, physical attention and I hated myself, thinking back on all those times I was so busy I pushed her aside—out of my den, but never out of my heart.

In her element in the mountains, she was a noble lady who belonged in front of stone fireplaces in rustic lodges.

We hiked many a trail and byway in the flatlands as well as in alpine settings and spent many a night sleeping together, the two of us under the stars.

I thought back on all the other good times we'd had together. Just she and I. We didn't need anything or anybody else. Nor did we need words to express our feelings for each other.

Through the years she had really gotten inside of me. So deep inside I could feel her in my heart and guts.

With the rain still coming down and the wind a bitter roar, I drove the flooded streets in ever–widening circles, my mind filled with wild imaginings.

What if she had fallen into evil hands? What if she were hurt? Maybe she would kill herself in an attempt to get away from her captors.

When darkness fell, I went home and phoned all my friends and relatives, asking if they'd seen her. I received much sympathy and some good advice which, I suppose, is common in matters of this nature. But none of this brought her back to me.

I had a cold supper in a gloomy house and the silence of the rooms was oppressive. Why did I need her so?

Finally, at nine o'clock, I heard a noise outside. I opened the door and there she stood, trembling amid lightning streaks, dog tired and dripping wet.

Frieda, my Saint Bernard, was home.

Airport Incident

The trouble with most airports is that there really isn't very much to do in them except wait to get on an airplane. Or wait for someone else to get off one.

Of course, there are restaurants and cocktail lounges. But how long does it take a person to eat a meal or drink a few drinks?

There are rest rooms but decent people don't loiter in them. There are book stalls and magazine racks but how long can a person browse standing up?

So you buy your plane ticket, check your baggage and that's about it. Then you wait and wait and wait.

If your plane is on time, there's no problem but what if you have a five–hour delay? When you start waiting, you don't always know how long the wait is going to be because often the departure time is reset. You don't know whether to take a chance and leave the airport or not. Not many people would want to risk missing their plane.

This was one of those times. Socked into the San Francisco International Airport in 1975 because of heavy rains and flights piled up six deep coming out of L.A., my wife and I trying to get to Honolulu to start an eight–day second honeymoon.

One thing I forgot. Besides those other things you can do, you can also people-watch. We were both doing plenty of that, too, along with intermittent napping as the third hour drug into the fourth and so on.

I first saw him at the adjoining ticket counter and our eyes met briefly and then passed on as stranger's eyes do, but there was something familiar about the guy. I saw him later alone in the coffee shop and still again coming out of a phone booth.

He seemed in a hurry. Just another black man in a hurry but there was something striking about this one. I knew I had seen him before somewhere but I couldn't remember where or when and it was starting to haunt me.

All kinds of people come and go in major airports and soon all the nationalities, races and costume apparels blend in as one sees turbaned Indians, tiny Japanese in kimonos, islanders from Hawaii and the Philippines.

But always my mind went back to the black man. I'd close my eyes and still see him. It was disturbing because I've got a pretty good memory for faces but a lousy memory for names.

Seats were at a premium and I was holding one for my wife while she checked our departure time for the umpteenth time when I saw him again. He was looking for a place to sit down. Then it came to me. He was a television actor and I'd also seen him in movies. Still, I couldn't recall his name.

Quickly, I grabbed my raincoat from the chair beside me and said, "Here, have a seat."

He thanked me and sat down, looking straight ahead. I turned to him and said, "I've seen you before on television, haven't I?"

He smiled, half rose, stuck out his hand to shake mine and said, "Yes, my name's Percy Rodrigues,"

It was at this point that 'I wondered just how I should handle this situation. As a writer, what angle should I go for? Should I blurt out that I was a writer and ask for an interview or would that only make him defensive? Should I ask for his autograph?

I introduced myself and of course I knew my name would mean nothing to him but then like an idiot I asked, "Is that your real name?" What I was asking was really, "Is that your stage name or is your name really Rodrigues." However, he said, "No. My real name is Percival but I prefer to be called just Percy. I spell the Rodrigues with an S, not a Z on the end."

There was a pause and I stammered, "My wife and I are going to Honolulu. She's around here somewhere—should be back in a minute. Where are you heading?" I was hoping to converse, to draw him out, to conduct an interview known only to me.

"I'm trying to get to Los Angeles. We've been shooting for two or three days here in San Francisco but the rains shortened my stay. It's been rough. I'll be glad to get back."

"I've seen you in lots or different kinds of shows on TV. I remember you on Dr. Welby and Medical Center and some cops-and-robbers' stories."

"Yes, I've been the good guy and the bad guy in those crime pictures. I've also been doctors, psychologists, and psychiatrists. I've even been in some Westerns."

Wishing I had a small tape recorder hidden on my person, I continued, "I think I've also seen you in jungle pictures as some tribal chieftain or something, haven't I?"

"Yes, there were some of those, both on television and in movies."

"You speak very eloquently and have great diction, no trace of any accent. Is that why you have been able to get such a large variety of parts?"

"Maybe. I speak English, French and Spanish. I was born in Toronto, spent most of my life up there. My father was Portuguese; my mother was French but I've had a French-Canadian upbringing."

I glanced out of the huge windows and through wisps of fog, the rain was still coming down. All the potential passengers sat glumly in their seats. We could see planes sitting silently on runways, none of them moving or revving their engines.

I turned to my unsuspecting interviewee and said, "Tell me how you happened to get into this line of work."

"Oh, I've been at this for years, I was just a kid when I started getting bit parts in summer stock productions in the East and we traveled quite a lot. I went to Europe and studied drama there, spent some time in the Shakespearean theaters of England. All that gave me stage presence and I learned to project and really learn to speak, actually."

"What do you mean by that, exactly?"

"Well, in Europe, outdoor theater is a big thing and of course, so is live theater but if you're not performing outside, you're in some massive opera hall and if you don't speak up, the audience will yell and boo and even throw things at you. That's the sad thing about George C. Scott. He is a tremendous movie star and winner of all kinds of acting awards but he really bombed in Europe because the people couldn't hear him and you know his voice is raspy and low anyway. It was too bad."

By this time my wife had returned from wherever she went after checking on our plane and was staring big-eyed at us because she knew Rodrigues was some kind of celebrity. She picked up my coat and sat on my left and I introduced the two. I knew she'd seen him before in the movies, also.

I asked Rodrigues, "Do you live in Los Angeles?"

I've just got an apartment there. J don't consider it my home. Canada is home to me but right now we're shooting a series in Los Angeles so I've got to get back."

All this time I was thinking what an opportunity I had here if only I was experienced enough to capitalize on it. No reporters firing questions, no mobs pressed close around that elegant gentleman, no bodyguards, no television crews with all their bulky, clumsy equipment.

My wife asked Rodrigues a question or two and remarked how she enjoyed seeing him on television, much the same thing I had already told him.

Suddenly, Rodrigues rose to his feet and exclaimed, "Well, I'd better check on my plane. It's been a couple of hours but it's a long way down that ramp."

I felt a surge of panic. What should I do now? I couldn't beg him to stay but my eyes must have been pleading something like (Oh please don't go. Stay, we've only just begun.).

But Rodrigues picked up his coat and a small suitcase. We shook hands again and he bowed to my wife. We wished him good luck and he wished us the same. I told him I enjoyed talking with him.

Just then a young girl, probably in her early twenties, rushed across the terminal to us and shouted, jumping up and down excitedly, "You're Percy Rodrigues, Percy Rodrigues. Oh, I'm so glad to meet you." Over and over she kept repeating it while he smiled patiently. He looked back at us once more before he waved and slowly walked away as the crowds closed in around him. The "interview" was over.

The Hospital Experience

I hadn't been a patient in a hospital for years. Not since I had all that tonsil trouble in the Army in 1953 and spent over 36 days in the military hospital at Camp Gordon, Georgia.

That occasion involved a bad case of infected tonsils and eventually a tonsillectomy. I was given a local anesthetic, sat up in a chair, and, in true Army fashion, they "cut those buggers out.'

This last incident was different. It seems I had impacted wisdom teeth which my dentist had decided must be removed because he had plans for some elaborate orthodontry and bridgework.

Getting into a hospital is not always easy. It's better not to go alone, both for psychological and morale reasons and also because two minds are better than one when it comes to getting past all the red tape and paper work.

For that reason, I was accompanied by my wife. Also, because I'm a craven coward. Of course, it is assumed that if you are an emergency case brought in through the emergency room in an ambulance with a screaming siren and flashing red lights, the whole process is simpler. They simply save your life, ask questions later and you are dismissed.

But if you walk in under your own power, you can figure on considerable delay. I sat in that tiny office for more than half an hour while the fat lady asked us all kinds of questions but mostly what kind of insurance we had and who was going to pay for the operation. At the end, she fastened an arm tag on my left arm, and I was amazed before it was over how many people consulted that band and all the information that was typed on it.

From there, we went to the lab. I approached a desk and the lady behind it asked politely, "Can you give us a urine specimen today sir?" I thought that was rather a personal question but I said I thought I could. She handed me a test tube and a paper cup and directed me to a restroom. I don't know why they call them restrooms because I don't believe one person in a thousand ever went in one of them to rest. Who do they think they're kidding? Everybody today knows damn well what a toilet is for. Also, some people call them bathrooms but there are no bathtubs or even showers in them.

Now, before I could even get up enough courage to enter the hospital, I had to have several drinks of strong spirits.

On that afternoon I drank three or four Scotch and waters. I usually drink Scotch and soda but I was out of soda and this was an emergency. Looking back, I did remember to fast but forgot I was supposed to drink only water before any lab work.

I went into the restroom and did my thing in the paper cup and then poured it into the test tube. On my way out, I turned and saw the directions for all these procedures printed on the wall. One set of directions for males and another set for females which I didn't bother to read but the poor dears had my sympathy.

I washed my hands and left. Another lady waiting outside snatched my still-warm specimen from my hand, smiled and motioned me to a chair in the corner. I made some remark about the urine specimen probably being invalid because of my alcohol content but she just laughed and said she also drank spirits occasionally for social reasons.

She stuck a thermometer under my tongue and took my blood pressure after which she told me she would have to have some blood. At first I thought she meant money but it was the real thing she was after, the stuff that vampires love and my heart froze.

As I recall, she took some out of my earlobe, my left index finger and from a vein in my right arm with the help or a six-inch-long needle. Through the pain and weakness of the loss, I wept.

I was assigned a room on the fifth floor and since I'm an unadulterated scaredy-cat, my wife went along. Of course she thought I was over-reacting but then she had three kids already so she knew what pain was. Also, women have a higher pain threshold than men do. Everybody knows that.

In the elevator was where I realized I was trapped and would probably never get out alive. The outside world was shut out and I was fighting the gnawing fear deep down in my guts that was slowly making its way to my surface.

From that point on, I was known as 537A. My roommate was 537B, a hernia patient who was up and around, already proud of his scar and acting smug because he had graduated from the worst of it. The pain, fear and trauma were over for him and he felt superior to me. I could see it in his eyes.

My wife soon left and then a nurse came with one of those horrible gowns with no back and told me to put it on. Then she said there was no real hurry since my operation wasn't until 1:30 p.m. the next day and I could get into bed whenever I wanted.

I walked over to the window and looked out at the view. The fall colors were beautiful and I thought of what a beautiful world it was. I looked down on the parking lot with all the cars and the doctors, nurses, patients and visitors moving back and forth.

Beyond was the city, the tree-lined streets, the mountains in the distance. I thought that it would really be a shame to die and not see all this ever again. It was so easy to feel sorry for myself and I hated that in me, the fact that I couldn't be brave. I hated my selfishness and my egomania.

I looked out that window a long time and just as the sun went down, an ambulance roared up and the attendants unloaded a gurney with an old man on it. I couldn't bear to look any longer and turned away.

For supper, they brought me the works: steak and potatoes and even a glass to the wine to my choice. The last supper, I thought, the condemned man's last wish, a decent hospital–cooked meal.

I spent the rest of my time reading, trying not to think about what was coming. And all the time the fingers or dread were clutching ever closer. It made me realize I really loved life and loved myself as well.

All night the nurses kept coming and taking my blood pressure and my temperature and in the early morning, the first shots right in my bottom, and I found it difficult to relax enough to let the needle in.

The anesthetist had come the night before and told me what he was going to do to me. I tried to be pleasant but found it hard to look him in the face. Who really wants to look at the hangman? I can understand why they wear a hood.

It must have been about 1 p.m. when a nurse came with more shots and all I could think about was how hungry I was without any breakfast or lunch.

The shots made me light–headed and somewhat cheerful. A different nurse came and she was smiling and giggling and I accused her of getting into the wine closet. After all, this was a Catholic hospital.

Soon a young Italian man arrived with a gurney and asked me if I wanted to go for a ride with him. Now only a fool or an idiot would actually want to go for a ride to a place where people were going to cut into some part of his body but I had no choice.

I lifted myself off the bed and onto the gurney and they folded my arms across my chest just like undertakers do, wrapped me in a blanket and we started off.

Into the elevator and down into the catacombs, darker with each floor, each gloomy corridor. Somebody grabbed my hand then my arm and looked at the armband. A voice asked me who my doctor was and what I had for breakfast. I answered and the voice said the answers were the right ones.

A door opened and I felt a chill. I said, "This feels just like a freezer in a butcher shop. I suppose that's to keep the meat from spoiling." Nobody laughed and I was wheeled to the center or the room under bright lights.

I raised my head and looked into the dark corners. The tables and furnishings were a sick green. Everything else was stainless steel.

People were moving about in that green world and they were green, also. Both men and women, dressed in surgical gowns, masks, and funny bootees, all in green.

I started telling a joke about three Italian prostitutes but my voice sounded strange, faraway Then, someone at my left said, "You'll feel a little pin prick." Someone asked me to scoot up on the table and I felt my head slide into a slot, my throat exposed. By that time, I knew I was in trouble.

Another voice behind me was saying, "What was that punchline?" and then a crash and a tinkle of glass and someone saying, "My God, was that what I think it was?" Another voice, saying, "Yes, it was. We'll all be gassed!"

The last thing I remember was the sound of someone sweeping up the glass. I woke up later in a recovery room but I don't remember going there.

Still later I woke again in the dark back in my hospital room with something wet running down my right shoulder and onto my arm. I reached toward my mouth with my fingers gingerly and felt the wetness. In the light from the hallway, I could see it was blood.

Two cylinder-shaped ice bags were wrapped around my jaws and both were covered with blood. My mouth was full of rolled gauze so saturated they were slimy and I was afraid I'd swallow one or choke on it. No pain but great numbness.

From out of nowhere the fat nurse came, helped me out of bed and into the bathroom where I jumped back at the sight of my bloody self. A victim of a chain-saw attack would look better.

I knew my backside was naked but she told me to calm myself because nobody else was up and moving around. Gently, she removed the bloody wrappings, replaced them with fresh gauze, and put me back to bed.

I awoke to bright sunshine later that day. The hernia patient had long since departed. So did I not much later when my wife returned to take a grateful me home.

On The Nature of Horses

Some people rave about how intelligent, gentle and noble horses are. My experience has been that the beasts are stubborn and unpredictable. Many of them have a strong horsey odor.

Now, I wouldn't know an Arabian from an Appaloosa nor a quarter horse from a Tennessee walker, but I do know they all burn hay and the expense of their upkeep makes them a bad investment for the average person.

Also, I think that except for the rock–hard guts of old–time cowboys and movie greats like John Wayne and Gary Cooper, the average guy's anatomy was not designed for horseback riding.

However, women and horses seem to belong together. Maybe that's why television commercials show pictures of young girls galloping graceful equines along beaches or across deserts. To see those beauties with their hair and the horses' manes flowing in the wind is indeed a spectacle that undoubtedly sells lots of shampoo.

And who could ever forget those scenes from The Desert Song with Margot in the arms of the Red Shadow after he and his band race across the sands in pursuit of those nasty Rifts?

Now my dislike for horses goes way back and let me relate what happened one summer a long time ago when my kids were really small back in the 1960s.

We were down in San Antonio, Texas, with a pack of relatives and they all had little kids. Well, all little kids and other innocents are crazy nuts about horses, so we had to take all those house apes to one of those riding stables where they had bridle trails and all the other accouterments for horses.

It was a sultry Monday afternoon and not a breeze was blowing there in Breckenridge Park when we all piled out of those station wagons and headed for the corrals.

Terribly hot. Terribly expensive, too, as I remember—about $2.50 per child for a half–hour. It killed the best part of a couple of twenties I was saving for liquor and cigars, but I anted up and didn't complain. Kids can be really persuasive when they turn on the tears and tantrums.

The women decided to wait in the shade and Jim and I took the job of escorting the kids. Now Jim is the guy who married one of my wife's sisters. They don't have a word for it in English but in Spanish he would be called my "cunyo."

Jim is a swell sport, healthy, strong, a transplanted Texan from Pennsylvania, over six feet tall and big–boned. He could pass for a horseman which is more than I could do.

Anyway, some hippie gal in jeans and pigtails came out and I gave her the tickets and she started getting all those kids ready.

She went around back and brought a bunch of horses up front. Now I mean horses, not ponies, and since this is Texas where everything is bigger that anywhere else, I mean these were BIG hoses. When I put my littlest kid up on the saddle of her mount, she looked like a flea sitting on the deck of a battleship.

When all the other kids were matched up with steeds, Jim and I were given a couple of nags and we all hit the dusty trail. Now, as I said, it was a Monday afternoon in the heat of summer and those horses had probably had the hell ridden out of them all weekend and wanted to rest so maybe that helps explain what happened.

I was on Sally, and from the first three steps I could see Sally had a mind of her own and wanted to set her own pace. Of course she knew the trail by heart.

As any jockey knows, a horse is a muscular animal, much stronger than a man, and any guy who says he has complete control over his animal is either stupid or a damn liar. But I knew Sally was in control.

All of this was bringing me bad memories. One I recall was of me as a toddler in diapers being pulled out from under a massive-footed plow horse. My parents told me later I had a hammer in my hands and was pounding on those hooves with it.

Anyway, I knew I wasn't a horseman, but when the girl asked Jim and I if we were experienced, Jim said like a true Texan, "You bet, I've had lots of experience around horses." I said nothing and just stood there like the craven coward I was.

Despite my attempts to hold her back, Sally took the lead at a fast trot which rubbed most of the skin off my thighs and took the crease out of my best pair of casual Levi flares. Through rocks and rills, woods and templed hills Sally forged on, stopping once while fording a stream to get a hefty gulp of water and let my legs get soaked.

About then, Jim caught up with me on his greatly undersized mare. I don't know why that girl insisted on giving the smallest horse to Jim, who was by far the biggest rider.

Jim seemed unconcerned about the whole thing even if his legs were dragging on the ground like Sancho Panza's. The tragedy of it was, I didn't feel at all like Don Quixote because I knew this was all an impossible dream!

Just as I thought I saw the kids coming behind us through the woods, Jim's horse broke out into a clearing and Jim said, "I think I'll see if I can make this horse run!" With that he dug his heels into the horse's belly, and off he galloped with Sally and me in hot pursuit.

Now all of us had received some brief instructions back at the stables, but the horses didn't, so when we pulled the reins to the left the horses didn't always go left but rather the way they damn well felt like going.

Sally wanted to follow Jim's horse and we sped on out into another clearing. All off a sudden, Jim's nag swerved sharply to the right and Jim flew out of the saddle and over that mare's neck.

Amazingly, Jim lit on his two feet and one hand in a crouch just as if he'd planned it that way—only he didn't! His glasses were knocked askew, and those horn rims really showed up plain on that red face with the crooked smile.

Well, Jim's mare, of course, ran straight back to the stables right past his wife who was sitting there in the shade. Seeing that empty horse and concern about the safety of her husband really turned her face pale and that's not easy to do since she's of Mexican-American ancestry.

I found out later the stable girl caught Jim's horse, brought it back to him and he remounted to finish the ride.

Meanwhile, Sally had broken into a gallop and I was almost back to the stables when I looked around and saw the kids all grouped up on their horses right in the middle of the arterial, blocking traffic. Who would believe engineers would run a bridle trail across a road? Running parallel with the road was one of those midget train rides that one sees in amusement parks. `Fortunately a train wasn't coming but it was interesting sitting there wondering whether it would be a car or a train that would wipe out our two families of kids.

Anyway, we all finally got back safely and that's the way that ended, thanks to all those patient drivers who decided to wait until the horses crossed the road.

The kids raved about how much fun it all was and what a good time they had. A half hour later Jim and his beast came loping up looking all calm and confident like he did this sort of thing every day.

Later that night, we all went out to dinner and Jim and I treated our wives to some great Pearl beers while we laughingly discussed the day's adventures. The children drank orange soda and Pepsi Cola.

The Conference Mystique

Many jokes have been told and many stories written about what goes on at conferences. A conference is supposed to be a place where people meet and "confer." However, experience often proves this not to be so.

A conference is really a place where people with similar and dissimilar interests come together for a few days of fun and frivolity. All this takes the form of staying up all night, the drinking of hard spirits, and a certain amount of hanky–panky.

Down through the decades in American culture, we have been taught that conferences are something that men and not women attend. Actually, conferences were merely excuses for tired businessmen to leave their wives for a relatively short time to kick up their heels in some hotel in a distant city. We now find the modern liberated female also attends conferences.

My most recent conference memory is of a three-day affair attended by writers, billed as a "creative experience," and held on a university campus in a neighboring city. This event happened in the 1970s.

Now writing is something that has always attracted large numbers of women and this conference saw the men attendees outnumbered about two to one by the fairer sex.

After three days and nights of mind-boggling speakers, workshop sessions, cocktail parties, dark- 'till-dawn informal gatherings with gin and tonic and good conversation, it is no wonder fatigue and giddiness sets in.

The culmination of the event was to be a champagne luncheon held at the Faculty Club with the keynote speaker being Rosemary Rogers, author of Sweet Savage Love.

I walked into the Faculty Club at exactly noon with another gentleman writer with whom I had been discussing the changing role of women in our changing society. We had both noticed that the women were coming on to the men pretty strong the last couple of days, and we felt it was just a sign of the times. He had remarked that this liberation was reflected in today's writings and a glance at any newsstand revealed that the writers of both genders had gone about as far as they could go. Of course, were talking about pornography.

He drifted off with some other writer acquaintance and I had just finished my first glass of champagne and was starting on my second. That giddy feeling, I referred to was just coming on when I felt a tap on my left shoulder.

I turned to see a young woman who looked like a combination between Liza Minelli and Barbra Streisand. She smiled and asked "Hey, are you a writer?" Because the champagne was really taking hold or me in the 90–degree temperature on that patio and because I could think of nothing else to say I said, "No, I'm a spy who came in out of the cold." She said, "Now come on, who are you really?" I said, "Well, in reality I'm a wealthy prince from a nondescript and mediocre kingdom with time on my hands."

She looked miffed and said, "Will you stop that and tell me who you are?" I said, "Okay, I'm a conference gypsy. I spend my summers just going from one writer's conference to another Who are you?" She gave me her name which I've forgotten, took my arm and sat us down together near one of the buffet tables. The rest of our conversation ran something like this:

Me: Well, I'm something of a writer. Just short pieces—a few short stories, some articles, a little nostalgia.

Her: (gushing) Are you really? That's exciting. I'm an essayist. They say there's no market for that sort of thing, but there is.

Me: You mean stuff like Henry David Thoreau, Emerson, John Locke and like that?

Her: No, my stuff is much different.

We both swigged down another goblet of champagne and just as the waitresses were getting ready to serve, she started looking cute to me, even sexy. For some reason, as I grabbed myself a meatball, I asked, "Hey, are you Italian?"

"No, I'm Jewish, a nice proper Jewish girl." Then she rubbed against me, winked and said, "Actually, I'm a filthy broad."

Me: Jewish, huh? Gee, I don't know much about that culture. I'm not even sure I like them. As you can see, I'm a WASP myself.

She: (rubbing against my thigh) Hey, I could really love you.

Me: But you don't even know me.

She took my hand, squeezed it, put her mouth to my right ear and bit it, saying all in one fast blurt, Hey, you're cute, you turn me my husband lets me date, I live right here in Palo Alto, yes, I would marry you, they're going in to eat, let's go.

She smashed her cigarette out on the concrete patio floor, jerked a compact out of a pocket of her pantsuit and hastily smeared on some lipstick.

Taking my hand, she pushed the two of us through over 372 people to a table in a corner, sat me down beside her and immediately clutched my left knee with long, painted fingernails.

Sandwiched between her and another woman who was going to dedicate her life to establishing a writer's colony in the foothills of The Sierra Nevada, I tried to eat lunch.

With both women chattering incessantly into both or my ears, I smiled politely first at one and then the other and was relieved when at last lunch was over and the mistress of ceremonies introduced the first speaker.

Many or the speakers were men but finally Rosemary Rogers came out. So, with the Jewish woman's hand on my knee and with the sensual and sexual voice of the beautiful Rosemary Rogers in the foreground, it was easy to rise to the occasion.

However, when the last speaker concluded along with the luncheon, the audience applauded, the Jewish woman rose to her feet and the crowd started moving to the exits.

I turned and whispered in her ear, "Well, baby, I guess the only thing yet to ask is, shall it be my place or yours?"

She smiled, shook my hand, said it was a pleasure talking to me and disappeared into the multitudes.

Why I Don't Ski Anymore

What possesses a person to put slats on his feet, venture into cold and possibly wet snow, zoom down a hill and go crashing into trees, rocks and people? I asked myself that question recently when I put on skis for the first time in more than forty years.

The only answers I could come up with were that a person is crazy to do it and that skiing is a dumb sport. I can understand people doing it if it is their job, such as members of the ski patrols who rescue lost, stranded, or injured people. Another example would be mountain soldiers in World War II who fought the Germans on skis across the mountains of Europe. And then there was Snowshoe Thompson who delivered mail to people in the Sierra Nevada and even packed a pot–bellied stove to somebody in the dead of winter. But to call skiing recreation is ridiculous.

It's easy to see why a lot of skiers don't even venture onto the slopes but simply sit in a lodge beside a cozy fireplace and get loaded on hot spiced wine.

Anyway, more than forty years ago, I was in college and a friend wanted to get me a blind date for a ski weekend at White Pass Lodge in the Cascade Mountains of Washington State.

Knowing my friend and his sick sense of humor, I fully expected him to fix me up with a blind date that was totally blind, probably 100 years old and, like me, unable to ski a lick.

Not so. The girl turned out to be a long-legged blonde Nordic beauty, a snow-bunny dream in ski pants and an accomplished skier.

But let me begin at the beginning. We arrived at the resort with everybody's gear attached to the car's ski racks—that is, everybody's but mine because I didn't have any. It was decided I would rent everything. As I remember, I was wearing long-handled underwear, jeans, work boots and a plastic raincoat.

A kid at the rental shed fixed me up with an ancient pair of skis which I swear were converted barrel staves with dried blood on them. I tried to ignore the gore and also the remark he made about being sure to fall down flat so when I froze to death I would be easier to carry out and place in a coffin.

I won't go into all the different types of bindings but suffice it to say in those days there were basically two types—cable and quick-release. Naturally, mine were not quick-release. I'd have been better off with just leather straps across my feet.

I stumbled out behind my date and the other couple; my breath caught in my throat when I saw the ski area. It was a cliff! They expected me to ski down a cliff!

Despite my protests, the three of them jerked me over to the ski lift. For the unfamiliar, let me explain ski lifts. You stand in a line with your skis on your feet, your poles in your hands and your heart in your throat waiting to be carried to the top of the mountain (cliff) in a ski chair.

However, we did not have the luxury of a chair, tram, sky chair or even a T-bar. We were expected to use a rope tow. Now a rope tow is a continuously moving rope which you are supposed to grab hold of and ski to the top before skiing to the bottom hopefully nowhere near that blasted rope.

Now, as a kid I had skied with an old pair of strap-on skis which afforded no control and on my last time out all those years ago, I had plunged down a slope and through a hog-wire fence. If that fence hadn't been rusty and therefore weak, or had been made of wood or brick, I wouldn't be alive today, recalling this tale.

Anyway, I grabbed the moving rope, almost had my eye teeth yanked out and somehow got the rope between my legs much to the hilarity of all onlookers. Soon I was rolling over and over, skis going in two directions tangled up with arms, legs and poles.

I got out of the contrivance somehow unhurt and plenty embarrassed and by this time my date was looking at me with a jaundiced eye full of misgivings and I knew I could give lessons on How Not To Turn A Girl On.

Anyway, the four of us gathered on top of the hill and they helped me collect my gear and we all started down. I was no more graceful going down and kept burying myself head first every couple of feet. The rest of the tale is too sad to relate except to say that the girl and I never saw each other again and my black and blue marks disappeared three weeks later.

And that's how I learned not to ski.

A Journey into No-Man's World

Probably every husband, from the seasoned veteran to the recent bridegroom, has felt the need at one time or another to buy his wife some fancy underwear.

The occasion might be an anniversary, birthday, holiday, or for no reason at all—except perhaps because the husband feels guilty over something or wants to smooth relations over after one of those inevitable marital arguments.

And then, of course, there are the times when the husband just wants to surprise his wife with a present when she least expects one. Most likely, he has given her candy and flowers so many times in the past that this time he wants to give something that will last longer than See's chocolate or fading Forget-Me-Nots.

Anyway, it was for one or more of these reasons that I sauntered into Rodericks of Burbank that day with the express purpose of buying some frilly lacy underthings for my beloved. Actually, the fact that Christmas was fast approaching must have had something to do with it.

Now, somehow a man always looks like a misfit in the ladies wear of any department store, but he appears even more out-of-place in a specialty shop such as this one which featured only women's undergarments and scanty swimwear.

I noticed there were a couple of other men in the store who cast furtive and embarrassed glances at me. Somehow their presence didn't give me the courage I so desperately needed at that moment.

At the time, I was standing spellbound before a scantily-clad mannequin and my lips were trembling, perhaps even mouthing some drivel to no one in particular. Small wonder those guys thought I might have flipped my gourd talking to a dummy.

Actually, I was merely stalling for time while I groped my pockets for the pair of white latex surgical gloves I always carry into "Ladies Wear." I've never liked to handle that frilly stuff with bare hands because it gives me goose bumps. Besides, since my hands are rough from gardening, I hate to take a chance on a hangnail or callus catching onto and ripping some of that fine lace and nylon. I'm certain some of those departments someday will probably have signs posted reading, "if you tear it, you wear it!"

Sure enough, by that time one or the salesladies had seen me struggling into the gloves and rushed over, probably thinking I was either the East Area Rapist or a vandalizing robber. Anyway, I had her attention.

Before she started screaming, I was able to blurt out my reasons for wearing the gloves and explain stammeringly I was looking for a present for my wife.

One of the men came over about then to explain that someone had torn the crotch right out of a pair of panties and they were therefore unsellable and should be removed from the counter.

He walked back to join his companion with a puzzled look on his face after the salesgirl explained the goods weren't damaged but were made that way on purpose for the sake of convenience.

Then she ignored my puzzled look by trying to show me everything she had in the shop all at once, including some jazzy garter belts.

The two of us started down the racks of this No-Man's World and into the aisles of the latest in swim wear, until we'd gone from the conventional to the traditional, from the sublime to the ridiculous, from the covered-up look to the string bikinis, from the maillots to the monokinis. Everything got more and more scanty and most of those bathing suits were no more than G-strings and could have fit into half a Dixie cup with plenty of room left over for a draft beer.

Then she showed me what they were wearing on St. Tropez and the Riviera this year, and to my amazement, it was two bottle caps and a cork.

About then, two strangers entered the store. I think they were men but it was hard to tell from the way they were dressed. One looked like some Italian lover from the Godfather or a sparring partner for Sylvester Stallone wearing high heels, lipstick and a bright pink leisure suit with the shirt open to the navel, revealing a blue bra and a lot of chest hair. The other was a pink–complexioned white businessman type with well–manicured nails and a lacy shirt.

They asked to see the baby doll nighties and I couldn't help overhearing the smaller one saying, "Hey, Gordy, I like this once. It's just my size and color."

The hairy one held the item up to his partner but winced when he glimpsed the price tag. "You know I love you, babe, but I'm not made of money, you know. Look around a little. See if you can't find something that costs a little less."

"Let's face it, Gordy, you're just a cheap tinhorn. I found that out when you gave me that engagement ring. That stone was so small, I had to look through a jeweler's glass to even see it."

The two kept arguing and bickering over the price of the baby dolls and haggled over other scanty "barely–there's." I dismissed the sales clerk and crept toward the door.

Then, for no apparent reason, my mind drifted back to a conversation I had long ago with a female school bus driver. She moonlighted as a salesclerk in one of those "specialty shops." Can't remember if it was Veronica's Closet or Frederick's of Hollywood. Maybe it was Victoria's Secret.

She told me that from her experience, many people of all sexes had a desire to wear some or this exotic stuff to fulfill some fantasy.

I put all that out or my mind and shuffled out and down the mall to the ladies' department at Sears. I felt sure I could find something suitable and inexpensive for my wife there. At least, it would be something that would keep her warm in the winter.

The Bear Saga

While camping years ago with my wife and three small daughters in Waterton Provincial Park, Alberta, Canada, I was faced with the prospect or fighting a 600-pound black bear from inside an umbrella tent in the middle of the night.

This memoir could almost have been called, "How To Fight Bare" but that would be untrue because I was wearing the bottom half of my long-handled drawers.

This adventure all ties in with examples of my poor judgment plus a lack of parenting skills, but I digress so let me begin at the beginning. Unless I'm getting two stories mixed up, we had planned on a two-week trip across seven states and two provinces in Canada.

Now, I've always been one of those guys who has to keep pushing further into the wilderness seeking solitude and beautiful, raw nature. That attitude can put people in danger.

We started out from Sacramento, stopping to camp at parks along the way to Seattle. Just out of Seattle, heading north, we ran out of gas. I left the family in our 1968 Volkswagen bus along the freeway and hiked a mile ahead to a gas station. That was the first example of poor judgment because it was my fault for running out of gas in the first place.

We proceeded north along the Campbell River in the twilight of the third day and it was soon dark and we still hadn't found a place to camp. Actually, we passed many campgrounds but I always thought there was a better one just up ahead. Perhaps all campers think that.

We must have crossed the border into British Columbia in the middle of the night and we must have stopped to show our passports to the guards, but I don't recall that at all. I was too wild and immature in those days to ask them where a good campground was. I was too macho to ask directions to anywhere.

The upshot was that we ended up in a largeroom above a barroom in a small town while rowdy drunks and a raucous band held forth beneath us for the remainder of the night. The room had one large bed, and my wife and the three girls slept in it while I spent the evening in a sleeping bag on the floor.

The next day we continued along the Campbell River where I kept an eye out for likely places to fish because I had seen all the signs showing huge fish which I suppose were Dolly Varden salmonoid or trout. I still didn't ask for information or directions because the people around there spoke mostly English or French. I never met anybody who could speak "American."

Anyway, we kept pushing on and eventually crossed over into Alberta. We drove into the town of Waterton about midday, and, of course, we forsook the luxury and comfort of a modern campground in town in favor of a more isolated spot a few miles out of town in Waterton Provincial Park.

I knew it was bear country but my family led me to believe they knew a lot about bears from facts learned in school—so why worry? Better to just enjoy any bears we might see.

My family imagined themselves experts on bears because in a previous summer we had seen them begging along the roads in the Grand Tetons and in Yellowstone National Park.

I lost count of all the visitor centers with their glassy-enclosed exhibits of all the types of bears and other western wild life, splendid examples of the taxidermists' art. The exhibits explained in great detail the habits and characteristics of the grizzly, the black, brown and cinnamon bears.

We had seen a female black bear and her three cubs just that afternoon walking through the heart of Waterton followed by throngs of tourists. She finally climbed with her brood to the top of a tall pine and ignored the gawks and camera shutter clicks. Another bear even brazenly walked into the front door of a clothing store on the main drag.

Yes, these bears seemed harmless, even funny, and the ranger that evening told us in his presentation not to feed them, scare them or otherwise molest them and they wouldn't bother us.

Again, I recalled from a previous summer a ranger in Glacier National Park issuing warnings regarding grizzlies. He said while in the back country never camp on trails or camp with a type or dog that might arouse a bear. These were two factors that contributed to the deaths of some people recently in the park. The ranger had concluded by saying it was also revealed that one of the girls in that group was menstruating.

Now, we knew a grizzly could be a threat but we felt safe because a grizzly had not been sighted in the area and we were not in violation of any of those rules.

The Waterton campground had everything we needed including hot showers and nightly nature talks. We set up camp and staked the tent down near the camp table and fire pit. The girls wanted to sleep by themselves in their sleeping bags in the VW and my wife and I decided to sleep in the tent.

It was probably around 1:00 a.m. when the two or us awakened by the sound of sniffing and heavy breathing right outside the tent. My wife calmly asked, "What's that noise? It sounds like some drunk guy is stumbling around in our area. "Then we realized it might be a bear.

Frozen with fear, we clutched each other, afraid to yell or make any noise. Now, I may be stupid but I knew that those sounds weren't coming from the lungs or squirrels, raccoons, or German shepherds.

Fearing the bear might come into the tent, I crawled in my underwear to the door, threw back the flap, and saw—Nothing! The bear had disappeared!

Nervously, we fell back to sleep but thankfully, our girls in the VW weren't even aware of what happened.

Anyway, I car camp with a grub box which I call the "Kamp Kitchen" and it's made of three-quarter-inch plywood with screw-in pipe legs, shelves and a fold-down counter.

That box was standing nearby in a small clearing, locked tight and when loaded with canned goods, it weighed at least sixty pounds.

As might be expected, the bear soon returned, rushed headlong into our camp, knocked pots and pans off the table and grabbed the grub box.

We rushed out of the tent, my wife remarkably "calm," the children awake and crying inside the bus. I jerked on the flashlight and saw the bear standing up and walking backwards with the grub box in his arms. That bear probably weighed less than 500 pounds but in my shaking flashlight's glare, he looked like a thousand-pounder.

I tried to remember all the things I'd heard about how to frighten bears out of campsites. I banged pans together until their bottoms were smashed flat. I jumped up and down trying to appear larger than I was and kept flashing the light in the bear's eyes. He just ignored me.

He looked grotesque. His arms hugged the box from which two of its four pipe legs, now broken, dangled uselessly. I was grotesque, too, jumping around in my long-handled underwear bottoms, a weak flashlight in one hand and a dull butcher knife in the other.

I kept the camp table between myself and the bear, realizing that we'd have a long and sleepless night if the bear broke open the box and tried to suck the contents from the cans. Also realizing that I might be an entree on his menu, I clutched the knife, determined not to die without a fight. My wife remained remarkably calm.

No help came and other campers nearby seemed to sleep blissfully on and, luckily, the box caught in the forks made by three small saplings and was stuck. Mr. Bear tugged, pounded, and pulled at it and though his teeth and claws gouged the wood, he couldn't move the box or get it open.

Discouraged, he left our area and we gratefully returned to our sleeping bags.

Bear damage is supposed to be reported. Next morning who should appear for my report but an attractive, immaculately uniformed female ranger! I hurriedly put my pants on while she listened almost unconcerned to my harrowing tale. That lady was as seasoned, cool and detached as any experienced male ranger would have been and had a cute Canadian accent to boot!

It seems Mr. Bear had made a few other calls that night, causing considerable damage and consternation to other campers.

While shaving later that morning in the restroom, a young man at the next sink told me that a bear had visited him, also, that night. More terrifying than our experience, he said that he and his new bride were on their honeymoon and camping in a tent trailer pulled by a small foreign sports car. It seems the bear wanted in and made his own hole in the screened canvas.

Apparently, the groom's blushing bride stopped blushing long enough to turn ghost white and leap toward a window. She missed and also made her own hole, almost being caught by one huge paw in the process.

The couple finished the night sleeping probably quite comfortably in their tiny Porsche since they were still married. And to think this all happened only a few campsites from us!

Well, we left Waterton later that afternoon and started back to California. But we decided to first visit my brother and his family in Great Falls, Montana.

On the way, I accidentally forgot to put my gas cap back on after leaving a service station. Realizing my mistake later, I stuffed a rag into the hole but it fell inside the tank. We had to have the tank drained somewhere in Montana. I never did get to do any fishing but we arrived okay back in Sacramento. But I was late and was penalized by my boss over that.

Perhaps I'm a camping nut but I'm getting that old restless wanderlust again. Probably I'll regret it but I'm already making plans for another trip next summer into bear country, probably someplace in Alaska. However, I'm leaving the tent behind and negotiating to rent a solid steel motor home for this sojourn.

And as Mark Twain's character Huckleberry Finn would say, "...I reckon I got to light out for the territory ahead of the rest..."

A Day on a Nude Beach

My eyes riveted to hers; we both sat naked on that beach and I was afraid to let my gaze stray and stare at her body as she explained that this was Black's Beach, the only legal nude beach in the United States. But let me back up and explain.

This was in August of 1974 and I had been attending a writer's conference in La Jolla. Another writer mentioned the nearness of a nude beach, and I was so intrigued I decided to stay over and check it out after the conference ended.

Was it for the sake of research and out or a writer's purely academic curiosity that made me decide to see what a nude beach was like or was it actually because I was just another dirty old man?

Anyway, I was in an upbeat mood, full of confidence after the seven-day conference and slightly stimulated and giddy, I set out to find it which I did!

Legal or not, Black's is not easy to get to. It's like they want you to earn the privilege. The longest way was supposedly the easiest down a winding asphalt road to a dead-end with no cars allowed beyond that point.

I took the shortest route—a rugged trail down a gulch with a twenty-foot drop near the last one hundred yards. This drop is negotiated with the aid of a rope suspended above with knots tied in it and hand-and-foot holes carved into the rock face of the adjoining cliff.

On top or the cliffs near the trailhead were homes overlooking the sea. Naturally, with all the bathers and spectators flocking in from all over to see naked people, these homes were constantly surrounded by automobiles and other vehicles. Even the maximum parking limits fail to deter the curious and no doubt many cars are towed away and impounded by the police.

About noon on a Saturday morning, I started down that trail with a six-pack of imported beer in one hand and a towel in the other because I thought a nude bather should show some class. But at that time I wasn't at all sure I would be a nude bather. Also on my person was a camera, a pipe, and some tobacco so I would have something to do with my hands if I did indeed decide to remove my clothes. I consider it greatly to my credit that I was not wearing or carrying a swimming suit.

After about a half-hour's walk, I went up a little rise and then made a sharp turn and there it was, a two-mile expanse of beautiful white carpeted with skin—skin that reached from the cliffs behind me to the surf and then north and south a mile in each direction.

The skin was all colors, all sexes, all ages and the panorama was broken only occasionally by a litter can or a sign reading, "Bathing Suits Optional." Overhead, hang-gliders soared peacefully among the seagulls. It seemed strange that with all this nudity around me that those hang-glider pilots were fully clothed.

A groundskeeper wearing only a golf cap and sandals moved among the sprawled forms picking up paper scraps with a pointed stick and stuffing them into a bag he carried.

As I strolled along, looking for an appropriate place to flop down, I wondered how old I was when I first saw a naked female. It occurred to me that I had never seen my parents with all their clothes off and that one can never completely know anyone until you see them in the altogether.

As I walked, I wondered what kind of people these were. Were they merely exhibitionists or sex maniacs? Or were they people just wanting to get a healthy dose of vitamin D or an all-over tan? Was there a relationship between nudity and actual sex acts?

I found a place not too close to anybody and spread out my towel. As I started taking off my clothes, I wondered what kind of a person I was and what my real reason for coming here was. Was it curiosity or did I really believe that by stripping off my clothes, I could strip off my inhibitions too?

Of course this was all years before those male bonding parties that are so popular today but I did feel the need to just go off somewhere and do "manly" things.

Amazingly, I found it quite easy to pile up my clothes, piece by piece, in a neat little stack and did so with only slight hesitation. It made me feel somewhat like a savage and I delighted in the feeling of freedom and lawlessness it gave me to be doing something that had always been forbidden by law.

I gazed around at all the bodies. There were shapely young girls looking for all the world like movie starlets with perfect figures and unblemished skin. There were lots of single men and there were families with young children and middle-aged women with suntan lotion and picnic baskets.

Because it was such a feast for the eyes, I found it difficult to relax at first but as the day wore on it occurred to me that this was perhaps just a re-enactment of fantasies.

In the dreams, you're always the only one that's naked in a street car or in a classroom and you wake up knowing it was just a dream but still feeling guilty and ashamed. Here was reality and these beautiful girls were not strip-tease dancers or on the pages of some girly magazine.

They were real and not posed and the fact that I didn't have to feel ashamed and fear arrest for indecent exposure indeed gratifying.

What does one do on a nude beach? I suppose first timers like me spend much time just walking up and down the sand but most of the others do the same things people do on other beaches.

Inhibitions would melt away when I would talk to other people. That's how I met this girl who is here with me now. Soon, we were splashing in the water together bodysurfing with the breakers smashing into our nude forms. It was good therapy.

Soon, we were busy tossing Frisbees with a mixed group of young people and found it thoroughly relaxing. We spent time in building sand castles and sculptures and just digging holes. Some people were covered with sand and all of us consumed some beer and wine during these processes.

The beach was large and without landmarks and soon I had no idea where my clothes were. I thought how difficult it would be to explain to a policeman in La Jolla that I lost my clothes on Black's Beach. Who would believe that?

I was told photography was not encouraged and could result in someone smashing your camera, so I refrained. However, one young man in a mixed group placed a girl in a model's pose and fired away. He used a Polaroid and we all saw the results of his work immediately.

Contrary to public suspicions, no hanky-panky was allowed on this beach. There was very little body contact but I did see one couple massaging each other and the application of suntan lotion was allowed but anything which constituted a lewd act was forbidden and could result in an arrest.

As on all beaches, litter can be a problem. Nude bathers can also be litter bugs. I found this out the hard way when I cut my hand on a piece of broken glass. It wasn't serious and one of the two young lifeguards bandaged it handily but I did have to give him my name and address supposedly for the purpose of statistics. Incidentally, the lifeguards were wearing swim trunks.

The biggest personal problem I had was not what one might suppose and it wasn't until later that I even realized I had a problem. That was sunburn! I had stayed on that beach so fascinated for more than ten hours, and the reflected rays from sun and sand had really cooked me. This was particularly bad because I had burned areas of skin that had never before been exposed to the sun, heat, and air.

However, with large amounts of Solarcaine, hot showers and plenty of rest in the shade, I avoided going to a doctor but did have to endure the annoying aftermath of water blisters and the inevitable peeling of huge hunks of flesh.

It was my own fault because all I would have had to do was ask this girl I was with to apply lotion to my naked body. I was just so shy and fascinated by her, I forgot to ask.

Others might have had some problems, also, but the therapy probably outweighed any bad effects. I remember one girl telling her friend that she loved to see people come to the beach and gradually lose a lifetime of inhibitions. I wondered if she was referring to me! She did explain that she was happily married but her husband couldn't be with her and that I was not her "type", whatever that meant.

That conversation made me wonder if a nude beach is for everyone. Could everybody handle it or would it really damage the sort of person that was taught that nudity was evil?

Is it all just a tease and sexually frustrating to see all these people of the opposite sex but not be allowed to fondle them? Could a person become so immune to nudity that the naked form of someone of the opposite sex would actually become unexciting?

All these questions I asked myself within those ten hours, but I really came up with no answers. I think nudity is an individual choice and fine for those who enjoy it. Some would probably never be relaxed with it.

I thought with a grin that what would really be a crowd-gathering sensation was if a woman showed up with three breasts or a man with three nipples or double his amount of normal equipment. Or how about transsexual or transgendered persons? Where do they fit in the mix? I don't recall seeing any.

I thought the people who weren't on the beach. Why weren't they there? Was it some emotional hang-up? Was it a fear of being raped or molested? Was it because they were ashamed of their bodies? Perhaps a bad scar, a disfigurement, an ugly birthmark? Too fat or too thin? Most or the people were quite good physical specimens, beautiful people, actually, but not all of them. A lot were average, few seemed to flaunt their wares; most seemed normal, at least by my standards of normalcy.

The sun sank into the ocean and cool breezes swept in. Time to start gradually putting on clothes and finally the inevitable hooded sweatshirts. Some couples were building fires.

Sleeping on the beach overnight was not allowed so the two of us dreamily made our way back to the path upward. I felt changed and wiser for having had a completely new experience.

Shasta Mountain High

If you have ever wanted to climb a high mountain, consider a volcano instead. Not Mt. Lassen but rather Mt. Shasta, a dormant volcano almost as high as Mt. Whitney.

Despite the popularity or backpacking because of improved equipment and freeze-dried foods, physical stamina is still an important requisite for mountaineering.

Unless a mid-week trip is possible, and depending on snow conditions, the three-day weekends or Memorial Day, Fourth of July and Labor Day could all be good for a conquest of Mt. Shasta.

Too much snow means floundering in drifts, making upward progress slow and laborious. Too little snow means crossing areas of sharp-edged lava talus which can cut hiking boots or get inside the boots and cause painful blisters. At any rate, unless a person is an experienced climber, do not go alone. At least two others make for a safer trip.

Here is a report of a typical climb: Fifteen members of a local mountaineering club have come from all corners of the Sacramento Valley to attempt the climb one long weekend. You meet with the others at 8 p.m. on Friday under the flagpole on the campus of Chico State University to receive a briefing from the leader concerning supplies and equipment.

The secondary meeting place is thirteen miles along the Everitt Memorial Highway at the 7,200-root Bunny Flat where you regroup and hike a short distance up to a Sierra Club hut called Horse Camp.

Because the facility is already filled with hikers, your people spend what is left of the night in your sleeping bags in the pastures outside. Of course, the odor of the nearby horses and their "road apples" is strong.

Equipped with freeze-dried foods, knapsack stoves, small nylon tents, climbing ropes, ice axes and crampons (spikes which attach to the soles of boots), you start the climb early in the morning. Your backpack creaks with the strain of the specialized hardware.

Once above the timberline, you look back on the small town of Mt. Shasta in the distance. All around you the terrain is dotted with cinder cones, evidence of past volcanic activity. You're walking in a world of red and black lava.

You're cautioned against drinking water from the runoff streams because such water contains microscopic silt which is too abrasive for the human digestive tract. Fortunately, some of you carry water in canteens which is shared with the rest of the party.

As you groan under the weight of your pack and sweat from the sun's heat, your feelings are best expressed by the woman member of the group who says, "This is a drag!"

You reach a plateau and before you stretches a treeless desert. It is a barren, dead-looking wasteland, but it is at least flat and a great relief after all that steep climbing. You see no animal life, and no birds sing as you struggle under your load. Still, it has a peaceful beauty in its aloneness.

By nightfall, you're high enough to be in snow which you gobble readily and drink the fresh water running out beneath the snowbanks.

You spend that night at a tiny glacial pool called Sisson Lake, nestled against the shoulders of the embryo volcano, Shastina. The lake is kidney-shaped and the reflection from the sky makes the water appear blue. This is to be your basecamp at roughly 11,000 feet above sea level.

In a silent world of ice and snow, you have supper and snooze in your goose down-filled sleeping bags for a much needed rest.

That Saturday night, temperatures reached below freezing, making it difficult to get up and moving the next morning.

While some of you receive instruction from Bob, our leader and his assistant, in the use of the ice ax and crampons, the experienced members embark on a short hike to the summit of Shastina.

At 11 a.m. you regroup for a briefing on avalanche dangers and survival techniques prior to our assault on Shasta. You are all wearing lug–soled boots and carry light lunches and a minimum of gear.

Roped together in teams of threes, you move across the snow fields ever upward, alternately crossing icy ridges and patches of bare red rock boulders.

Sunglasses reduce the glare from the snow and you feel secure after one of the Swiss alpine club members trusses you up like a Christmas goose at the end of one of the three–man teams.

The leaders goad on the stragglers and you know time is important because storms can come up unexpectedly or a deadly "white–out" can make it impossible to see in any direction. Running out of daylight can also be a problem because to hike in darkness is foolhardy.

All of the natural beauty or Northern California unfolds behind as you sidestep around crevasses and cornices along Whitney Glacier toward the summit.

A moving river of ice and snow, Whitney Glacier exists year–round and is one of the largest of the five glaciers on Shasta.

Though afraid at times and all your physical senses keenly alive, you feel confident the other two climbers can hold you if you slip into a crevasse.

For hours you grope upward across the ridges and snowfields until finally, one by one, lungs bursting, you reach the rock–bound cluster of lava which marks the summit.

Breathlessly, you sign the steel–bound register book and take pictures of each other, feeling proud that you have accomplished something that not everyone can achieve.

You have climbed 14, 162 feet above sea level to the top of the most dominant peak in Northern California to behold the thrilling panorama below Mt. Shasta, the southern-most peak in the Cascade Range.

To the north stretches Oregon and to the south the vast expanse of the Sacramento Valley.

Under the September sun, the wind screams around your ears, and you are further awed by the sight of looking down at the top of a commercial passenger plane as it flies beneath you.

You huddle together, hugging each other and drinking wine, making toasts to the victory. You have not arrived by the easier tourist way but have taken one of the more strenuous mountaineer's routes instead.

You feel like a conqueror but it is written somewhere that people don't conquer Mt. Shasta. You are only permitted to walk on her. Many Indians consider her sacred and some people have claimed to have seen ghosts and even the famous Sasquatch or Bigfoot, on her slopes.

Descending from the summit soon after was anticlimactic but sheer joy because different sets of muscles are used.

In base camp that night at Sisson Lake, as you sit eating dehydrated steak and drinking more wine, you can't help thinking what a glorious thing it is to climb a mountain.

Withstanding the relentless buffeting from the winds, surviving the dangers of the crevasses, and finally reaching the pinnacle, a feeling of possession as well as conquest overwhelms the hiker.

It makes you want to scream out that this is your mountain and your land because you are strong enough and skilled enough to succeed. Such is the sweet taste of triumph and another reason why men and women climb mountains.

Notes From A Backpacker

On a rainy night in the spring of 1959, I attended a Sierra Club meeting in the Garden and Arts center in McKinley Park in Sacramento, California.

Having heard about the Sierra Club and some of its activities from friends, out or curiosity, and as a lark, I attended the meeting alone.

The program for the evening had already started and the room had standing room only. The keynote speaker was David Brower who has since died, but on that night I had no idea who he was. I knew nothing of his fame as a mountaineer, conservationist, author or any of the rest of his outstanding accomplishments.

He had been addressing the group and I had the feeling he had just finished his speech when he saw me come in, rain dripping from my windbreaker. He paused the question and answer period, asked me my name and inquired about my interest in the Sierra Club.

I said, "I really don't know much about the Sierra Club and actually, I just came in to warm up and get out of this cold rain."

The crowd roared with laughter but Brower didn't miss a beat and answered, "Get that man's name and sign him up. Don't let him get away even if you have to lock the doors."

Thus began my relationship with that organization that lasted over twenty years and I've never regretted joining it.

The Club's purpose has always been to "explore, enjoy, and preserve the Sierra Nevada and other scenic resources of the United States and..."

In those days, however, it seemed like we members were mainly concerned with the enjoying and exploring of the wild places, and we seldom got involved with the politics of protecting and saving those areas. I was as "fun hungry" as anyone else and after I became a member, I did lead some trips and even held the lofty position of Assistant Day Hike Chairman of the Mother Lode Chapter. To me, all these activities were the closest thing that modern men and women could come to adventure.

The members voluntarily joined the activities they most enjoyed which were broken into categories like Day Hiking, Backpacking, Peak Climbing, Rock Climbing. Car Camping, Trail Maintenance, Campground Clean-up, and later, River/Gorge Scrambling. Of course there were offshoots from these categories like fishing, photography, swimming, gold panning, and rock hounding. Even then, some trips went to other countries.

Also, getting off in the wilds away from cities makes some people feel really free and they "go native", let it all hang out by going nude and other crazy uninhibited doings like that.

One trip that stands out in my mind was that August adventure with about 30 members into the Selway-Bitterroot Wilderness area of Idaho. It's a remote place and includes the refuge of a North American elk herd and even further north than the ramous Sawtooth Range in Idaho. The Selway-Bitterroot Wilderness area has been aptly described in Norman McClean's short story, "The Ranger, The Cook. And a Hole in the Sky".

I recall kissing my wife and daughters goodbye on that sweltering hot day in my 1963 blue Volkswagen bus which I affectionately nicknamed, "Superwhale." This was sometime in the 1960s.

My destination was the trailhead in the Lolo Pass area on the border between Idaho and Montana and I went north through Nevada, Oregon, and Idaho as the small towns and the paved roads petered out. As I recall, this was to be a one-week journey.

It was to be a Campground Clean Up and our mission was to locate and clean up old forest service camping grounds and dumping pits by bagging the cans, bottles, metal and trash in burlap bags and hauling them out aboard pack mules.

My companions at the trailhead had arrived in two army surplus trucks complete with all the cooking supplies and food. They were a mixed bag, most of them barely young adults, the youngest around sixteen and the oldest in her sixties. They had all met at their starting point in Berkeley, California.

I had reached the trailhead near Voodoo Like over a dusty rough bumpy muddy road and got stuck once getting there but my new companions easily pushed the old bus out of the mud. From there we had to hike fourteen miles into Lake Isaac where we would set up our headquarters for a few days. Then the plan was to move again into the West Moose River Country. At this juncture, I wondered where the mules were.

The trail itself was rough, steep and almost non-existent in places. Our packs were heavy and a lot of stream fording was required. Top-heavy with all that gear made it difficult to keep from falling over backward off the narrow log bridges. I couldn't help but wonder how the sixty-year-old lady fared.

Our leader was a nineteen-year-old volunteer fireman from Berkeley named Steven, a very mature individual for all his tender years and his assistant leader named Tim from Chicago. Our cooks were two charming girls around eighteen years old, accompanying us as a guide and amateur counselor was a forest ranger stationed in the area. I can't recall his name but I do remember he had a large black dog with him.

Hot and exhausted by the time we reached Lake Isaac and hours ahead of our pack mules, I did succumb to reckless abandon and impulsively threw off my clothes as well as my pack and waded into that cold water stark naked. I looked back to see nobody else was following my lead, and I felt like a fool, especially after all the others saying they were going to do likewise. I merely assumed they would, like me, be going in au naturel. I guess that was because this was in the 60s, the time of the hippies, nudity and flower children. I was older than most in this advance party and none of them were female. Strange, though, that in all that heat, none of the other guys even went into the water.

Later, after I was out of the water and dressed, three of the young men and myself stood side–by–side fishing off the lake bank. I was using a mosquito fly; the guy next to me was using salmon eggs and the other two guys were using various lures. Within a half hour, we had enough trout for the entire party's supper that night. It seemed each cast from any one of us caught a fish, all of them at least eight inches long. Shortly thereafter, a summer rain blew in and that ended the fishing. All we could do was seek shelter under the evergreens and wait for the main party and the stragglers.

The others all arrived in the late afternoon with the ranger bringing up the rear along with a few mules laden down with the cooking tents, food and other gear. I think some of the mule packers helped the leaders and the cooks set everything up and the hot meal we had that night was greatly appreciated by all after eating nothing but cold trail mix all day. We spread out and set up our individual tents and sleeping bags in a level clearing sheltered by a few trees.

The next morning, I woke up to see a bunch of mules carrying gunny sacks happily chomping grass in the meadows and after breakfast, we started out with some meager tools to search for and clean up campgrounds. I recall seeing many rusty bent bean cans and lots of White Horse whiskey bottles. The packers loaded the mules and were moving some of them out by mid–day.

After the first few days, I thought we knew each other pretty well, but still the boys and girls used separate swimming holes although we did fashion a community toilet which was just a hole in the ground with a toilet seat over logs.

The project was nearing completion when it was decided we would not move our main camp but instead start early one morning and hike into the West Moose River country, taking only a few tools and two mules. We found it to be pristine, beautiful, and primitive with clear water and roaring rapids topped with white caps. We did find and clean at least one campground which had more White Horse whiskey bottles.

The cooks had prepared bag lunches and it was a long day for all of us that volunteered for the West Moose. It was dark before we got back to the main camp.

Then came that strange experience. It seems the pack train had forgotten two items, canned peaches and toilet paper. An air drop was arranged by the ranger with his "walkie–talkie."

That afternoon I was on my way to the latrine when a girl told me she wanted to show me something. She took me by the hand and pulled me into her tiny tent. She showed me a picture of Jesus, pulled out a marijuana joint, and lowered her jeans. She wore no underwear. Then, she pushed me back and climbed on top of me. Suddenly we heard the roar of a small plane and people shouting and running. I could hear the pack animals nervously milling around.

The girl rolled off me and yanked up her jeans. We left the tent and silently watched as the merchandise parachuted down. Even though I held her hand, I was secretly relieved. It was hot inside that tent.

Nature in the Raw

Hiking and backpacking were two of the most popular forms of outdoor recreation in the 1960s. However, other pastimes have developed as off-shoots of these activities. Today's visitors to the wild places spend their time at such pursuits as fishing, climbing mountains, photography, rock-hounding and many other sprightly activities but I wish to discuss lesser known ones here.

Also, it's only natural that some of these visitors have their own secret places and mine was a pristine campground on a river four miles from the nearest trailhead.

Though I hadn't hiked to the place for several years, I nevertheless felt possessive about it because I knew I could do practically anything I wanted to do there unheeded in solitary freedom.

It was mid-summer and I left the scalding city with my heart full or anticipation and enthusiasm. My Kelty was full of dried foods, pack rod, swim fins, mask and snorkel and a swimming suit—all that was needed for a weekend of aloneness.

Excessively warm even in the foothills, I headed into the higher elevations and was at the trailhead by noon.

To my astonishment, I met others on the way in—some guy on a trail bike, a horseman and a couple of bearded young men with gold-dredging equipment.

In the hottest part or the afternoon I reached my Shangri-la and started setting up camp on a bank a few yards above the river.

I was amazed to find I was not the only camper. In fact, I learned I was adjacent to a lean-to constructed by and occupied by eleven Boy Scouts and their fearless scoutmaster.

On my right was a battered picnic table beside a crude fire pit. Five packs and several sleeping bags on top of the table reserved the site for its absent tenants.

I took off my waffle stompers, put on moccasins and set up my small two-man mountain tent. While I was unrolling my sleeping bag, I caught a glimpse of bare human flesh through the trees.

A young girl emerged from the brush and into the clearing of the unoccupied camp on my right. She wore no shoes and everything above the belt of her blue jeans was naked skin.

Now I've been in topless bars and to burlesque shows and have seen nudie movies and magazines before so I know what little girls look like. Besides that, I'm married, but out there in all that nature I stared in disbelief.

Terrified that the girl's eyes would meet mine, I nonchalantly continued unpacking, tripping over a log and noisily scattering my cooking pans hither and yon.

Not fifty feet from me, the girl casually walked to a mirror fastened to a tree and started wrapping her hair in a bandana.

In case the girl was watching me also, I figured it only fair to take off my shirt. While removing the shirt, I knew it was only a male ego thing which wouldn't make any difference.

Usually I can set up camp in less than thirty minutes but this time I was finding it unusually difficult. It was maddening to try to rig my clothesline and prepare my fishing equipment when my eyes kept swinging back to that half-nude girl who was as unconcerned about my presence as the rocks and trees.

Thoroughly disturbed, I took out my worn copy of Thoreau and tried to read. Unable to concentrate, I put on my boots, picked up the fishing gear and decided on a hiking and fishing excursion along the river.

Making a looping trek upstream, I found quiet pools filled with trout. In the heat of day, they stayed down deep and I caught only the inexperienced ones that were too small to keep. I could see big trout below and was frustrated to see they wouldn't take any kind of lure. I tried eggs and worms to no avail and decided to try again at dusk with flies. Donning my swim trunks, I spent an hour or so swimming.

Returning downstream, I neared camp only to find the tranquil silence shattered by the presence of three or four of the Boy Scouts perched atop huge boulders noisily throwing rocks into the river.

As I passed them, they giggled and shouted at me not to go any further. Not fifty yards from me on a sandy beach I saw her. The other girl back at camp was a blonde but this girl sprawled on her hack on the sand was completely nude and completely black-haired.

Knowing I had to get past this girl to get to my camp, a number of problems confronted me. Of course, the uppermost question in my mind was the age-old one of What Do You Say To A Naked Lady?

I had put my shirt back on for the hike but now I felt a compelling desire to stop and remove all my clothes and leave them in a neat pile on the beach. Suddenly I felt inferior and awkward. Out of place. I was the outsider with the gall to appear fully clothed while nature's creatures existed happily without all the trappings of civilization.

And not the least of nature's creatures was this girl, so slim, firm and beautiful, round in all the right places. She belonged in this natural wilderness more than I did. I fancied myself an outdoorsman but I was the misfit, the ugly pollution that spoiled the landscape.

But my puritan upbringing lost out and I decided to approach the girl as if I was accustomed to frequently seeing naked women on remote beaches.

She hadn't seen me yet so I circled around in front or her trying to act casual and said, "Hi, I saw you lying here and wondered if you were injured or something. "It must have sounded stupid and I immediately regretted saying it but she sat up and looked me full in the eyes.

As I engaged in small talk, I noticed she seemed uncomfortable and must have felt vulnerable lying there because her intent stare seemed to say, "Why don't you look me in the eyes when you're talking to me?" I was looking her in the eyes because I was afraid to let mine wander but somehow it was different and very difficult. Could she be reading my mind? What was she thinking about?

She told me she was with a party of four others and one of them was injured. She pointed to the water and I followed her unpainted fingernail to the water's edge where I found a nude man behind a boulder with his left foot in the river.

The guy told me he fell off the trail while hiking in and he thought he broke his ankle. I told him I'd try to get help and thought perhaps the scoutmaster would have some pain-killing drugs that might help reduce the obvious swelling.

Trudging back upstream, I finally found the scoutmaster in the middle of the stream in his waders busily engaged in teaching three or four of his protégés the art of fly casting.

I shouted to him about the injured man downstream who needed attention but he replied that he didn't even have an aspirin, so I retreated bewildered and dejected.

When I returned, the injured guy and the girl were gone and one of the Boy Scouts nearby told me a group of trail bikers came in, rendered the necessary first aid and carried the guy out.

Overheated from my exertion I continued downstream planning on another swim.

Rounding a bend, I was startled to see a young boy and girl nude in the sitting yoga position midstream on a huge boulder in the pool I had planned for my swim.

Awestruck at the beauty and naturalness of these sun-worshippers, I half regretted being without my camera but felt that perhaps a picture of this would be another obnoxious intrusion from civilization. To interrupt this tranquil scene in any way seemed to me sacrilegious so I quietly slipped away.

Venturing a little further downstream, I removed my clothes and donned my swim fins, mask and snorkel. As I entered the water feeling more free and natural than I had in my entire life, I looked back to see the couple on the bank waving at me as if I had their permission. Their camaraderie was a tangible thing and it made me feel welcome.

Later, back in camp, I slept fitfully and because the night was warm, I returned again to the river for a late night nude swim.

Moonlight bathed me as I entered the water but I discovered I wasn't alone. On the rocks all around me were the five from my neighboring camp. They silently joined me in the water.

Thoroughly relaxed, we all swam together without false modesty I thought how ridiculous convention was. In a movie we probably would all be wearing masks and feeling inhibited under stage lights but this was no movie, only stark reality.

Perhaps the act of stripping away garments enables people to strip away prejudices and pretentiousness. At any rate it's relaxing therapy, and I returned to my sleeping bag renewed and refreshed. From this experience I learned that nothing is predictable when finding yourself in a place which is lost to civilization.

Looking Back at Vanishing Wild Places

Looking back on over twenty-five years of backpacking, exploring, hiking, and camping, I decided in April of 1972, to write down some of my observations.

The great majority of people in the United States have never seen a true wilderness. Many of today's children may never see one. Thousands of people camp, hunt, and fish, or otherwise "go to the woods" but most of them do so in marginal areas near cities or in the various state or county parks. To the purists, the only way to see a true wilderness is to either hike in or follow a wild river by kayak, canoe or inflatable raft.

It's debatable whether a true purist would even consider pack animals as compatible with a wilderness experience. Horses and burros can truly wreak havoc in a fragile alpine pasture if not in small numbers and carefully controlled. Also, hiking close behind them promises to be an unsavory expedition.

The idea of wilderness may appeal to many people but most seem to derive all the nature lore and "roughing it" their souls demand from a small city park, a vacant lot or green belt in the heart of giant cities.

Modern folks go to the wilds for many reasons; the trophy hunter learns about the best places to go for a shot at a record-size animal, the fisherman has his favorite stream and the rest of us all have our beautiful little secret paradises we'd like to think are known to us alone. We go to these places for many reasons and we'd like to think they're honorable reasons, and maybe they are.

Anyway, in my opinion, this was one of the reasons two schools of thought developed. Some of the early conservationists and others who lived in the wild places and loved them adopted a possessive attitude and believed they were the ones that knew how to appreciate the wilderness and take care of it.

The average homesteader was afraid of nature and fought it viciously. On the other end of the spectrum, we had the exploiters, the vast number of peoples who felt nature was something to subdue and they saw little beauty in it, only economic gain.

However, an exploiter in one man's opinion might be a preserver in another man's mind. It can be easily reconciled either way. Probably, exploitation results in jobs.

Many early Native Americans and their chiefs believed that the land and its resources were a gift from God, meant to be used, loved and shared by all. They didn't believe in trading it or selling it. This idea was impractical, of course, and the whites with their idea of Manifest Destiny soon stole most or the land from the Indians and started setting up claims and homesteading rights.

There are still some conservationists, I think, that have these selfish ideas but most are enlightened and in educating the public to protect, enjoy, and explore wild areas of the world. I say "wild areas of the world" because we still have those who are concerned only with certain regions such as the Sierra Nevada, or the American West, in general, at the exclusion of areas in foreign lands that are in need of protection. The word "protection" is what concerns ecologists, environmental activists and conservationists, and brings me to the subject of problems with people.

Assuming that a wilderness is a large, roadless area which may or may not have rare plant and animal life, perhaps certain types of people don't belong there. I can readily understand why some of us prefer animals to people.

I recall seeing on one trip fifty or sixty boys fishing shoulder to shoulder on the edge of a tiny glacial lake trampling delicate vegetation and later, after catching undersized trout, throwing fish entrails up and down the shores.

I remember, after laboring for hours to the summit of a nine-thousand-foot peak, watching two boys and a girl trying to change that beautiful landscape by rolling boulders down the slopes of that mountain. And yet, to them, it seemed as harmless as skipping a few pebbles across some quiet lake.

Assuming again that a true wilderness bears no mark of man, I shudder when I think of the dozens of temporary shelters, lean-tos, and toilets I've seen constructed out in God's country where the builders used huge spikes and nails as well as nylon lashings to make their fastenings. Naturally, those devices were left there to help the next weary travelers.

And then, of course, there's the litter and garbage seen around primitive campfires. I've found horse people and fishermen among the most frequent violators. It follows that since a horse can carry more than a man, some pack stock is made to carry heavy canned goods as well as much bulky, unnecessary equipment and personal items such as portable television sets and transistor radios.

Not wanting to carry empty cans back out and thinking that burying them will eliminate the problem forever, some people do just that and also bury bottles and other non-burnables. Some common ones are pop-tops, bottle caps, tinfoil and those plastic six-pack holders, just waiting for some bird to get it caught around its neck. These seem to always end up crumpled and thrown into the campfire.

Then, there are the collectors. It has been said that wilderness travelers should take only pictures and leave only footprints. Some photographers take pictures but leave their film wrappers or film containers scattered about. The ancient philosophy of taking, not giving, still prevails way out there as witnessed by the multitudes who can't resist picking wild flowers, digging up plants and trees, gathering rocks, chasing and/or killing snakes, squirrels or other animals. Why is it that some people can't just photograph or observe animals without having to kill them and mount their heads?

To me, over seven people in a group in the wilds is too many but if in a remote area at least three is necessary for safety reasons. Small wonder that the truly competent and knowledgeable people prefer to go alone. Examples would be John Muir and Ansel Adams.

We have been taught that there is safety in numbers but this can be disastrous to Mother Nature in certain places. Research is being conducted to see how many people can be accommodated in these areas, for how long a stay and for doing what kinds of activities. I've seen large groups of boys completely strip small conifers for their boughs to sleep on, completely decimate ground cover, hack trees for fun and catch over their limits or rare trout, most of them undersized.

The toilet and garbage activity alone of fifty boys in one spot for a weekend is sufficient to pollute a small lake or stream for a season. Some boys' groups seem notorious for washing their dirty pans in lakes and streams and throwing the residue and detergent back in the water. Also, it isn't difficult to imagine the clattering and noise pollution a group that size can make.

Many people unknowingly pollute, and today the battle lines are drawn between the polluters and the nonpolluters, the exploiters and those who strive to practice sensible approaches to the environment.

The so-called "cowboy" philosophy that we've inherited from the Westward Movement is apparent in the methods or many modern lumber barons. That is, when the lumber or any other resource is gone from an area, they simply move on to another lush stand. Our country is running out of lush stands and this attitude sort of ties in with a lot of experiences I've had with men, machines, and roads.

Man, in order not to only fight and subdue wilderness, which he has always considered his enemy, has employed machines to help him. This carries over into his recreational pursuits as well as aiding him toward greater economic wealth.

Small boys grow into men in the twenty-first century believing that there is something manly about machines and have grown accustomed to the noise and pollution they create.

It was natural, then, that the roads that penetrated the wild places should be used later for four-wheel drive vehicles, trail bikes, and snowmobiles.

So much damage has been done by these vehicles to trails, especially in the wet season, that they have been banned from many areas. One would imagine by now that someone would invent a silent gas-driven vehicle because the noise from them can be deafening. However, the manufacturers and dealers are making big profits, creating jobs in designing these large toys, and like everything else, powerful lobbies exist in their favor. Politics are everywhere. It's only a matter of time in America before we have multi-use recreational areas because everyone must do his own thing and have his sport yet many sports are not compatible with one another.

One time I came upon a fat man astride a Tote Gote alongside a trail in a remote canyon. The vehicle had broken down and its rider had no way to repair it. The thought immediately occurred to me that this man was so badly out of condition that his heart could fail him on the long hike up and out. The vehicle was far too heavy to push or carry. Did it occur to the salesman or the buyer of the vehicle that such a thing could happen? The man left the vehicle and started out.

Another time I was snowshoeing into a tiny hut in the middle of nowhere, thoroughly enjoying my privacy and the serenity of the woods in winter. I heard what I thought was a chainsaw but coming up the hill in my tracks was a skier holding on to a T-bar pushed by the smallest motor imaginable. In his wake floundered a tiny dog, whining so pitifully, the skier finally picked him up and tucked him inside a pocket. My impression was that this must be one of the laziest men I'd ever seen because he turned the machine around and had it push him downhill also!

The point I'm trying to make is that most people will do anything to keep from being self-propelled.

As I see it, roads, and particularly improved roads, brought many men and many problems. No person has all the answers. There is no one answer, and we're discovering that we don't even have all the questions yet.

Conservationists are in a minority, but there are thousands, probably millions of exploiters. If the purists in the environmental movements had their way, would they want us all to squat like Indians around primitive fires, trap our food and live of the land? Could modern man do that? Thoreau tried to do it for two summers at Walden Pond and he did it only with the help of friends who took him into their homes on weekends. Still, how can millions of people live off the land today?

It seems to me the conservationists and other brainy persons in the world should pool their knowledge and intelligence and come up with ways to make a living off of nature without destroying it. Thus, exploiters have always been realistic and have seen their work as noble because it enabled people to have jobs, feed their families, create wealth, live in physical comfort and improve their status among their peers.

In conclusion, following all these arguments for and against man's need for jobs versus nature, I personally feel a sense of loss and longing for what once was, and still is, important in my life, the beauty of the changing and slowly disappearing true wildernesses especially in the American West.

How Not To Kill a Cat

Everybody who knows me knows that I like animals. In fact, I like animals better than most people like them. Also, I like most animals better than I like most people.

I have had animals as pets most of my life. They were usually dogs or cats of the mongrel variety such as Ralph, that outcast black cat I had when my daughters were little.

It would be difficult for me now to have to shoot an animal or even spank one because I'm such a softie. That wasn't always the case if birds and fish could be roughly classified as animals/pets.

Yes, I thought nothing of blasting away at upland game birds with my 16 gauge Stevens shotgun or yanking some trout out of a lake and whacking it hard in the head while the blood flew. Thank goodness I never had to kill a deer or any other game animal to ward off starvation.

We had all manner of critter in the house while I was growing up and later with my own family, we had chipmunks, squirrels, white rats, guinea pigs, hamsters, and even chickens and goldfish.

But now I want to write about Juice. His full name was Orange Juice or O.J. which had no connection whatsoever with the infamous O.J. Simpson, ex-football star and acquitted murderer.

No, Juice was a huge orange domestic shorthair tabby cat with big eyes and an independent streak. He looked somewhat like

Garfield from the comic strip but I don't recall Juice ever showing an insatiable hunger for lasagna like Garfield does.

But let me tell this story which might not have had a happy ending except for the stupidity of people and the great common sense of this antisocial feline.

Now, Juice wasn't my pet. He belonged to my ex–wife, Pamela, who had been told by her apartment manager shortly after she moved in that pets of any kind were not allowed on the premises. She would have to choose between staying in an apartment without Juice or finding an apartment that would allow small animals. However, even then, Juice was not a small cat and probably weighed at least seven pounds.

It was springtime and that may have been one of the reasons why Pamela must have lost her senses and all reasoning ability because she had decided that she and Juice must part because she could no longer keep him.

Therefore, she called an organization that is supposed to prevent cruelty to animals and explained her problem to that association. They assured her that they would do everything they could to find someone who would adopt Juice and give him a good home.

I didn't realize at the time but later came to know that springtime is the season for "cute baby kittens" and Juice would be competing against these kittens for a loving home and also just to stay alive because at that time in the 1990s many animals were still being euthanized.

Pamela cajoled me into taking Juice out to the affiliation's headquarters in south Sacramento. With the help of our adult son, Thomas, we finally crammed the cat into his traveling cage which he hates and on a windy, chilly day in March, we put him in the back of my pickup and headed out with Juice meowing and scowling at us from his wire prison.

We pulled off the freeway and into the parking lot of the place and carried Juice in his cage into the office. I told the woman behind the desk we were leaving this cat off for adoption. As I recall, I was clutching his rather impressive papers, license, shot records and all that other crap pet owners must have.

145

The woman told us we had to take Juice out of his cage and put him into one or their cages which was considerably smaller. Now, Juice is a muscular animal and while we tried to make the transfer, he jumped out of his cage onto the counter, then onto the floor and scooted behind a Coca–Cola machine.

Two big men were summoned from the back rooms and manned with long-handled nets and brooms, they tried to poke and otherwise convince Juice that it was not in his best interest to try to set up housekeeping under the soft drink dispenser.

Finally, Juice ran out and into an adjoining room, both men in hot pursuit. The men finally cornered him and brought him back in a net and set him up on the counter again. They both wore long sleeves and leather gauntlets for protection. Of course, there were not scratches on the men, not even on their merciless faces. Part of the reason because Juice had been declawed in his not so distant past but there he was, dusty, ruffled, spitting, snarling and growling. His ears were flat against his head, his eyes were merely slits, and his fur puffed up so that he resembled a bobcat and seemed every bit as big as one.

Thomas and I moved closer to the counter, hoping he'd see us and take some comfort in our nearness and calm down. But he would have none of that and as the men tried again to ease him into the smaller cage, he tried to bite through their gloves and squirm loose.

As I moved closer, his fangs looked six inches long and the woman said, "Sir, do not attempt to touch that animal."

Suddenly, a lump rose in my throat and seeing Juice's plight, knowing he would probably be put to death within the next two weeks, tears came into my eyes and I yelled, "This is outrageous. Forget it. I'm taking him out of here."

Somehow, the men got him back in his own cage without hurting themselves or Juice except for his dignity and we took him home to my place.

Since I had a little terrier dog at the time, I knew they had to be separated so I put Juice in my bathroom with rood, water, and his litter box.

Once, while the dog was outside, I let him out of the bathroom and, as I sat reading in my recliner, I caught him looking at me from the hallway with one of his big yellow eyes, a sinister, angry, fearful yellow eye.

He stayed with us for about ten days, I think, and after Pamela found a suitable animal loving apartment, we moved him back in with her.

Juice lived many years after that, fat and happy but she was the only one he ever really trusted. I marveled at the way she could grab him off the floor and hold him upside down like you would a baby. It seemed to me she could play with him or do anything with him she wanted to do.

When I would visit, he usually gave me a wide berth and I couldn't help feeling guilty about how I had been a party to his near execution. Also, I had helped use up one of his nine lives.

The End

www.ingramcontent.com/pod-product-compliance
Lightning Source LLC
LaVergne TN
LVHW040151080526
838202LV00042B/3114